A Time To Be Born...

EARLVILLE FREE LIBR.
EARLVILLE, N.Y.

By BRIAN VACHON / Photographed by JACK and BETTY CHEETHAM

PRENTICE-HALL, Inc., Englewood Cliffs, New Jersey

A Time To Be Born . . . by Brian Vachon / Photographed by Jack and Betty Cheetham

Copyright © 1972 by Brian Vachon and Jack and Betty Cheetham
All rights reserved. No part of this book may be
reproduced in any form or by any means, except for
the inclusion of brief quotations in a review, without
permission in writing from the publisher.
Printed in the United States of America T
Prentice-Hall International, Inc., London
Prentice-Hall of Australia, Pty. Ltd., North Sydney
Prentice-Hall of Canada, Ltd., Toronto
Prentice-Hall of India Private Ltd., New Delhi
Prentice-Hall of Japan, Inc., Tokyo

Library of Congress Cataloging in Publication Data
Vachon, Brian, date   *A time to be born* . . .
1. Evangelistic work—California. 2. Revivals
—California. 3. Youth—Religious life. I. Cheetham,
Jack, date,   illus. II. Cheetham, Betty, date,
illus. III. Title.
BV3774.C3V3   269'.2'0973   75-37623
ISBN 0-13-922039-9   ISBN 0-13-922021-6 (pbk.)

Design by Janet Anderson

The young man was gaunt-blond, trembling slightly, his strained face and close-cropped hair saying pretty clearly that he had recently been to war, and had picked up a communicable disease of that war—heroin addiction. Under his arm, he had a fatigue jacket and two army blankets. He stood alone in the back of Bethel Tabernacle —the squat, white Pentacostal church in Redondo Beach, California, where miracles are supposed to happen.

He looked dazedly toward the front of the church, at a scene almost as unreal as anything he had seen in the service. There were young people—some kneeling on the floor, some sitting with their backs up against the wall, others crouched over the church's movie-theater seats— and they were praying, praying in tongues.

It is an eerie sound to someone who has never heard it —like loud, garbled, unintelligible wailing. "Oh Jesus Jesus alababalabalabalabal noilabanoilaba balabalabala- bala Jesus Jesus Praise you Jesus thank you Jesus."

A roomful of people were energetically, earnestly babbling—hands extended into the air, heads tilted back, tongues moving furiously in their mouths.

Then one young man slowly rose from where he had been kneeling and picked his way through the sprawled congregation to the ex-serviceman in the back of the church.

"Welcome, brother." A hand was extended, and tentatively, briefly accepted. "You're welcome here."

"I'm on smack and I want to get off. Someone told me at the airport that you guys can help me."

"Jesus can help you."

"I don't know anything about Jesus. I know about smack. And I want to get off!" A slightly desperate edge framed his voice, and he was shivering almost violently.

"What are those for?" the welcomer said, pointing to the jacket and blankets the young man was holding now with both hands against his chest.

"The sweats."

"Forget it. You don't need them. You need Jesus, in your life, now, right now. Want to try to ask him into your life? Do you want to ask Jesus to be your personal savior? You know, that's what he wants you to do."

"I don't know. Yea. I'll try it. I don't know."

"Try it. Just ask Jesus to come into your heart."

The young man slowly knelt down and faced the huge, bare wood cross at the front of the church. "I don't know who you are, Jesus," he said with a voice soft and jerked by his shaking body. "I don't know who you are and I don't know if you even exist. But if you're there, man, I really need you. I'm not kidding, Jesus, I really need you. And I want to accept you and know you, man." The voice was growing louder and the other young man knelt down and put his arm around the ex-soldier's shoulder and started softly praying also. "Oh praise you Jesus, praise you Jesus. Please help this brother who is asking for you right now. Thank you Jesus. Thank you."

But the ex-serviceman was beginning to pray louder and his shaking was now violent. Others in the church rose to their feet, drifted back, and knelt around him, some putting their arms on his shoulders.

"Jesus I really need you. I mean I really need you: Please help me Jesus. Oh God, please help me Jesus."

The others around him were now praying furtively, some in tongues, some in English. "Praise you Jesus, praise you Lord. Praise Jesus." It was a prayer with a rhythm, seemingly increasing in tempo. "Praise Jesus. Oh help this brother, Jesus. Thank you, thank you, thank you Jesus."

Louder and louder, faster and faster, the praying was becoming intense and more intense and suddenly the young man doubled over as if he had been shot in the stomach. With his fists beating the floor he shouted out, "God! Oh God, please God! Please, please Jesus." And then he was sobbing freely and helplessly. The others were now all praying with their faces lifted up toward the church's flat white ceiling. "Thank you Jesus. Thank you Lord. Oh thank you, precious Jesus."

It was all over in less than a minute. The young man's sobbing gently eased, almost as if mesmerized he began to join those surrounding and supporting him in the simple prayers of thanksgiving. "Oh man! Oh Jesus, thank you. Oh Jesus, wow! Thank you."

After a few moments the group rose to their feet with the young man still looking obviously stunned, and tears still running down his face.

"Welcome brother," someone said, and embraced him solidly. Then others were hugging him and each other and shaking hands, laughing, praising God. The young man now was smiling, still dazed but no longer trembling. As he was embraced, he kept looking around the church, looking as if he had never been there before, saying in a voice of half reverence, half disbelief: "Oh wow. Oh man. Man, thank you Jesus. Thank you Jesus. Thank you."

Bethel Tabernacle's famous thirty-second heroin cure had worked again. The guarantee of no withdrawal agonies, no sweats, no pain if you accept Jesus Christ had been fulfilled. One more thoroughly surprised but completely convinced member had been added to Bethel's rapidly growing, spreading, dispersing congregation.

But the cure is not confined only to Bethel and the converts are not made only in California and the accelerating phenomenon, media-dubbed "The Jesus Movement," is not merely passing adolescent obsession. It is the most infectious spiritual revival in the history of this country. And according to the new Christians, the last.

I want to write about this revival, but write about it as a reporter, not as a theorist. So I will write only about what I saw and heard and a little about what I felt while watching this revival grow. I looked at the Jesus Movement in California, where—like freeways and drive-ins and motion pictures and everything else new to catch some national fancy during this century—I believe the Movement began. This all had to start in California. It has California stamped all over it.

That's speculation, I suppose, and I'll try to make it the last piece of speculation in this book. But I can't resist the urge to pinpoint the beginning of the movement, and so, not quite arbitrarily, I'll say it started in the Haight—San Francisco's celebrated Haight-Ashbury district which basked in a brief flicker of human fellowship in the spring of 1967.

"Everybody was moving there, trying to create a new society of some kind," explains Ted Wise, 34-year-old veteran of the Free Speech movement and subsequent rebellions, and then director of the Drug Abuse Center in Palo Alto.

"We wanted a society based on love instead of greed and deception and political scheming.

"But something bad happened. We had brought the old world in with us. It's like when they send a space capsule to the moon, they're extremely careful to decontaminate it—kill off all clinging germs and viruses.

"When we moved to the Haight, we hadn't been decontaminated. We brought with us everything that corrupts the world. I myself had been using drugs for eight or nine years, but at first, most people weren't. There was genuine concern for the world's problems. But the more people became involved in drugs, the more the concern turned inward.

"By the end of that first summer, we were beginning

to know that something was wrong. Nothing was being accomplished. Concern for others and the world's problems disappeared. Drugs that were shared at first became a matter of greed. People were murdering for dope, just like they had in the outer world.

"That was where Jesus came in," Wise says.

For Wise, the first encounter with this personal savior business was provided by his wife Liz—an uncommonly beautiful and gentle mother of two who had brought her own share of "the world" when she moved to the Haight.

"I was raised in a real Christian family, but at a very early age I rebelled against everything," she said. "I needed attention, affection, physical appreciation. That's why I gravitated toward Ted. He was a very sensuous man. He could provide that in my life."

Ted and Liz got married, had two children, fought a lot, started smoking grass pretty regularly, and eventually graduated to LSD every weekend. "It petrified me, but it also gave me some hope—hope for something better in this world. And it taught me something—or reminded me of something. It reminded me of the reality of good and evil. I realized for the first time in years that there was no hope trying to live apart from God.

"I started going back to church and I really felt like God was pulling me closer and closer. I was getting very turned on about the Lord, and things were getting together in my head.

"Ted was awfully uptight—mad at me most of the time, but I knew he really loved me, he really did. So I prayed for him a lot. I guess it was kind of half-hearted praying, though. I kind of hoped he would be saved some day, but I couldn't see it in the near future.

"Then he started reading the Bible, and I thought, wow! I was delighted, because I hadn't asked him to read it or anything, but I was scared. There wasn't going to be any middle ground. He was either going to tear it up and reject it forever, or believe it and become a zealous Christian. That's the kind of man he is. There couldn't be any in-between."

While Liz was telling me this, sitting at her country kitchen table and talking with her peculiar and delicate animation, I felt as if I was listening to a mildly subdued faith healer's undercover accomplice. It was all too-good-to-be-true-stuff. Two beautiful and intelligent people slipped off the straight and narrow and lived for a while in hell on earth. But then they found God and lived happily ever after.

But here were these two beautiful and intelligent people, talking about Jesus Christ as matter-of-factly and present-tensely as they would talk about a next-door neighbor. And they were two people who radiated happiness, and contentment, and peace. It showed all over them. So when Liz gave me the predictable end to her fairy story, I felt a little as if my common sense was being tampered with. "One day Ted came to me and said he had accepted the Lord. And immediately I knew he meant it, and I knew what kind of Christian he would be. He was going to be the active kind, and I could dig that.

"But for weeks after he accepted the Lord, I was walking around in a daze. I believed it, but it was too good to believe. It was like we were really married for the first time. We loved God together and we loved one another and grew together. It was beautiful."

"That was a few years ago," I said to Liz. "How about now? Are you happy?"

She simply said "yes," but I have never been so sure of an answered question in my life.

Ted and Liz Wise joined with three other Christian couples and decided to form a Christian commune. "We were thinking Utopian ideas," Ted said. "We wanted to have our own place far out in the country where no one could get to us and we could cut ourselves off from the rest of the world. We put an ad in the paper saying 'large Christian family needs home' and we found one in Sausalito. We all moved in together—eight adults and seven children in a two-bedroom house. It was a situation where prayer and faith in God's will was an absolute necessity."

The four men in the commune divided their time between working odd jobs and conducting street ministries. Eventually, they opened a storefront on Haight Street—furnished it with a folding table, half a dozen chairs, and a huge bowl of fresh soup daily. The soup was the bait. Hippies in the area were getting hungry, living on love.

"We used to sit around a table every evening and make the soup," one of the wives in the original commune recalled with relish. "During the day we'd go around to the butcher shops and get scraps of meat and bones and we'd go to the produce markets and get the stuff that was too old to sell. But it was too old because it had ripened—it was perfect.

"Every night the soup we made was different. We'd prepare the meat and vegetables and put them into the bowl and then let it all simmer on the stove over night. The men would take it to the mission the next morning."

The soup became legend in Haight-Ashbury in 1967 and probably got a lot more attention than any results from the tiny mission. "But kids who were just like us, maybe some younger, would come in off the streets and we'd feed them and tell them what Christ had done to our lives.

"We never had to preach to anyone about free love being something that didn't work. They had already seen the heartbreak and jealousy that develop from it.

"But we just talked about Christ and the Bible. Some people were receptive to it. Of course some would be receptive to anything. People would come in and want to hang up their political thing right away for *anything*. They come out of a radical background and say, 'Yea, good. We'll become Christians. Great.'

"That kind didn't last long."

But other kinds came into the mission during the two years of its existence—thousands and thousands of other kinds, hungry kinds and curious kinds and the desperately seeking kind. Wise and the others were preaching a kind of Christianity that many of the young people hadn't heard about before. It was specifically nondenominational. It was taking spiritual responsibility out of the hand of ministers and priests and giving it to everyone. Some of those who stopped in at the mission were picking up on what the young ministers were saying. And many, of course, did not.

"I talked to Charles Manson almost all day once," Wise said. "He came into the mission with about four girls. He was a kind of normal-looking chap, but he was very cold. His attitude was cold. I thought he was a speed freak. He wasn't open at all to what we were trying to say."

But enough others were. Seeds were being sown. Many of the new Christians I talked to said that at the moment they decided to accept Christ, they would remember something someone had said to them maybe months earlier: something that really didn't stick at all in their minds at the time. Some would remember a phrase some minister had intoned from the pulpit during a church attendance of their childhood. Others might recall the urgings of a street preacher they had walked away from a year ago. If there is a continuing theme in the witness of young Christians, it is that something they heard a while back—something they brushed off and ignored—suddenly came back and became lodged in their consciousness.

I can't help thinking an awful lot of those kinds of thoughts were first planted in the mission on Haight Street. Sociologists say the Jesus Movement sprang up simultaneously in a number of places on the West Coast as young people searching for hints of immortality were blindly susceptible to the promises of Scripture. Ted Wise would be adamant about giving credit where credit is due ("It's God doing it, and anyone who gets the goofy notion that a human has a hand in it has his head out of shape. We're just doing God's work").

But just to satisfy a selfish and possibly unreasonable desire to make things concrete, I'd say that the initial thrust of the Jesus Movement came from the mission on the corner of Haight Street, and billowed out like an uncontrollable underground explosion.

I first heard about the Jesus Movement from my agent. He told me that two photographers—a husband and wife team, Jack and Betty Cheetham—had left his New York office one fall afternoon, declaring they were going to California "to find the Jesus People."

"Uh-huh," I said. "More power to them." At that time, I should add, the juxtaposition of the words "Jesus" and "People" was a new one—at least to me.

"Not so fast," my agent said. "They've found them."

"Uh-huh."

"They say they're all over California. Young kids toting Bibles and spouting Scripture to anyone who will listen."

"Great."

"And *Look* magazine wants to do a story about them with you writing it and the Cheethams taking the photographs."

My agent had suddenly hit me where I lived, and the matter of young people accepting Jesus as personal Lord and Savior suddenly became a subject of great personal interest.

"When do we start?"

"Immediately."

"I'm off," I said. But I wasn't really in quite that much of a hurry. I didn't want to go off completely in the blind. I called Jack Cheetham in California.

"I hear you announced there was a Jesus Movement in California and you were going to go and find it," I said.

"That's just what I said," Jack answered. "Betty thought I'd really flipped out. She didn't know what I was talking about. It was all news to her."

"But you found it," I said, looking for assurances. "This so-called movement."

"Yea, brother. I found it. Praise the Lord!"

Oh, lovely, I thought. I've got a fat magazine assignment, and I'm pleased about that; and I'm going to California, which is nice. But doing a story about a bunch of Bible-thumping kids? And with a pair of photographers who run around saying "Praise the Lord!" I was suddenly mighty leery.

"There's really a revival out there?" I said.

"It's bigger than anything you can imagine," Jack said. "Hallelujah!"

"Okay, tell me something honestly so we can all know where we stand. Are you in on it too? I mean, Christ-as-personal-Lord-and-Savior, and all that?"

It was funny hearing those words come out of my mouth. When I was a kid, hitchhiking in the South, those were the words I most dreaded. When guys would pick me up and get into that, I'd either immediately think of a reason for getting out of the car, or gird myself for a long, nagging sermon about how hot hell is going to be. And it seemed like guys who picked up hitchhikers were always into the Jesus thing.

But this was a business question, and I was going to have to know sooner or later. "Have you? Accepted Christ as your savior?"

"Yes. We suffered over it, then we made our decision."

"Both of you?"

"Yes."

"Okay . . . See you in California."

"So long. And praise the Lord."

"Yea. So long."

I went out to California, and the Cheethams picked me up at the airport. The first place we visited was Melodyland, a mini-astrodome in Anaheim that was once a 5,000-seat theater for touring Broadway shows. Now it was a

huge religious complex. The cocktail lounge had been converted into a rehearsal room for the choir, and the dressing rooms were used for Bible classes.

The pastor of this huge church is Ralph Wilkerson, who looked—when I first saw him—like the pastor of a California religious complex called "Melodyland" should look. His tie looked silk, and he handled his hand microphone with professional deftness. I couldn't tell for sure, but I was betting he was wearing expensive cuff links.

It was a Thursday night—a scheduled evening service—and of the 5,000 seats, about 4,800 were unoccupied. Those that were filled held mostly middle-aged or elderly people. When they sang "Holy, Holy, Holy" with mechanical reverence, I couldn't help thinking of the little Methodist church my mother attended, where people fanned themselves not so much to keep cool as to keep awake.

Following the hymn, Ralph Wilkerson took the stage. "Do you remember the first time you ever said 'Praise the Lord'?" he asked. "Do you remember that it sounded a little strange? And didn't you kind of think people would make fun of you?"

"Aaaamen," the congregation responded woodenly.

"And now it just kind of slips out, doesn't it? It's spontaneous."

"Amen."

"Kind of makes you feel good, doesn't it?" Wilkerson said, his voice friendly but unmistakenly authoritarian.

After completing his short sermon, Wilkerson invited the congregation to give witness—"to share with others what the Lord has done for you."

A 73-year-old minister from Tijuana came up and said the Lord had healed him of arthritis, but now he had hardening of the arteries.

"Pray for this good man, friends," Wilkerson said, and two hundred heads bowed obediently.

Then a young man came to the front and told how he had received the Lord and it was like being "hit with a bucket of love." Wilkerson stepped next to the man and said he would pray with him. Then, directing his eyes downward, he asked the Lord to take special care of the man because he was a special person. As he spoke, Wilkerson's voice grew increasingly intense and he slowly raised his hands just above the man's forehead.

Then he touched him lightly, and the man fell back like a tree—straight down, flat out. But when his head was about a foot and a half from the floor, someone from

the front row (an assistant pastor, I found out later) leaped up and caught him under the shoulders. The man lay still with his eyes closed for a few moments, then got up—dusted himself off—and returned to his seat.

Following the young man's testimony, half a dozen other people—generally middle-class and middle-aged—came to the front and told a story of how they had been blessed, or needed blessing. And they were prayed over by Wilkerson and then touched and then kayoed and then caught.

This, I was thinking, is not any part of a revival. This is a guy with a gimmick and there have been guys with gimmicks ever since religion began. The next thing you know, they're going to take up the collection.

The next thing I knew, they took up the collection. The audience dropped bills into the velvet baskets that were passed up and down the aisles while singing, rather appropriately, I thought, "He Touched Me."

For the next week, the Cheethams took me on a whirlwind tour of the Jesus Movement in California. I saw hundreds of new Christians—mostly kids—clean and glowing and

constantly praising the name of the Lord. I saw an ocean Baptism where the newly baptized emerged from the water with a radiance on their faces that was almost staggering. I attended evening prayer services where hundreds of young people crammed inside a small chapel to sing and pray for hours into the night. I saw heroin addicts literally lose their addiction while they were praying for help. I saw kids—hippies and surfers and bikers and cheerleaders and every kind of kid you can imagine—carrying Bibles, all bursting with some newfound spiritual energy.

And it didn't take much time in that week for me to get thoroughly convinced. Yes, there was a great new Jesus consciousness in California. It wasn't small or isolated. It wasn't the latest trip. It seemed to be a full-fledged revival. I was ready to go back to New York to write about it, and if people thought I was crazy, the Cheethams had the photographs to prove I wasn't.

I only wanted to clear up one thing in my mind, and that was the service in Melodyland conducted by Wilkerson. Everything else I had seen seemed so genuine, and yet so many people had told me Pastor Wilkerson was truly an inspirational evangelist. I was able to speak to

him the last morning I was in California—a Sunday morning between services—and I told him that the evening I had watched bothered me—that it seemed like huckster stuff.

"To be quite honest," he said, "the overt supernatural is the only thing that can turn many older people on. They are often attracted to things they can't understand.

"There are too many passive churches in the country today. They're boring people to death. We're getting people excited about the Lord."

I wasn't sure I understood what he meant, but if Wilkerson's way was part of the movement, that was fine with me. The important thing was that a spiritual revolution was going on in the West that a lot of people didn't know about, and I was going to write about it.

Which is what I did. And a lot of other writers did also. Within not too much time, every major magazine and every major network had given the Jesus People their scrutiny. And we were all pretty much saying the same thing. It's big. It's growing. It's sweeping the country. Jesus is invading popular music and the Broadway stage and causing ecstatic behavior everywhere.

But will it last? Will it last? Will the movement come,

convert a few thousand Christians while gathering millions into a passing bliss trip, and then move on? And will it then leave the millions more strung out than they were before? Will the Jesus Movement last? Is this it? Is this the fulfilling of the prophesies of the Old Testament and are the last days of the world at hand? Is the Second Coming around the corner with these legions of young people bearing witness to the Light? Or is this just one more burst of religious energy in a country whose history is filled with revivals?

I suppose time is eventually going to answer those questions. But I was very interested in knowing what a little bit of time had done to the new Christians I had first interviewed. I wanted to know how their Christianity had held up under the glare of national publicity and after twelve months of Amening it up. And I also wanted to see how the Movement was going in other places.

I first went to Berkeley where I was told that Christians who had been converted several years ago were bringing new converts in by the hundreds.

Across the Bay, the Haight-Ashbury district was a grimy ghetto of boarded stores and littered streets. The place where I speculated it all started was not where it was happening now. But in Berkeley, Jesus seemed to be very much alive and well.

Jack Sparks, a bearded, deceptively businesslike ex-statistics professor from the University of Pennsylvania, is something of a catalyst for the movement in Berkeley as well as counselor to young Christians.

"We came to Berkeley because we felt it was the vortex of the changing youth culture in America," Sparks said. "By and large, kids all over the country look to Berkeley. We came with the concept of the apostle Paul. 'When I'm with a Jew, I act like a Jew. When I'm with Gentiles, I act like a Gentile. When I'm with the heathen, I act like the heathen. But I'm just doing this to get the good news out.'

"We came with just that concept in mind. We weren't going to try to change the culture here. We're just going to try to add something to it. The person of Jesus Christ."

Sparks and his wife started their Christian infiltration of Berkeley by opening their home to students.

"We lost that house because the neighbors didn't dig us at all," Sparks says, smiling. "They didn't like all those freaks around. They didn't like the fact that we had prayer meetings on Monday nights. We started with just a small family study group called 'Bible raps.' At the last one we had, there were almost two hundred people in our living room. The neighbors didn't dig that at all, so we lost the house."

Sparks found a new home for his enlarged family, and helped establish other Christian houses in Berkeley and a Christian ranch commune nearby.

I attended one of his Bible raps, and this one had at least two hundred participants, ages seventeen to seventy. The uniform was generally tie-dyed T-shirts and jeans, with a sprinkling of Afros and plenty of bare feet. I was struck with the remarkable ethnic balance in the room—like a sit-down strike at central casting—Chicanos, blacks, straights, hippies, orientals, Latins, young and old.

The session opened with singing led by a delicate, pale girl named Jeannie, who sat huddled over her six-stringed guitar in the front of the room next to Sparks. It was announced that she would soon be leaving Berkeley to return to her home in Chicago and attend Bible college. She blushed as people in the room expressed unhappiness at losing a cherished "sister." But that meekness disappeared when she sang, and she filled the room with a strong, mellow soprano.

I was told later that Jeannie had been literally carried into the Christian house less than a year earlier, suffering from malnutrition and drug overdose. She had been one of Berkeley's street people—deadened and aimless. That picture of her would have been hard to imagine, watching her smile, close her eyes, tilt her head back and sing

Trust in the Lord with all your heart
and lean not upon your own prudence.
In all the ways, think on Him,
and He will direct your steps.

After several songs—standard hymns as well as restyled folk tunes—Sparks spoke to the group, a soothing semi-sermon that combined street language with Scripture.

"You, Jimmy, and you, Foxy, and you, Shelley, and all of you in this room and all Christians everywhere. We're all joined with him and with each other. Look around. Those are your brothers and sisters. We're joined by the Spirit and we all have a special role to play on this earth.

"Thank God for Ephesians 2:8, 'For by grace you are saved by faith, and that not of yourselves. It is a gift of God.' And then later in verse 19, 'Now therefore you are no more strangers and foreigners, but fellow citizens with the saints and of the household of God.'

"Man, I really praise God for those words," Sparks

said, and almost every head in the crowded room nodded enthusiastically, and fingers were drawn down upon Bible pages to find the text that had been read.

"God gave us a clear understanding of who we are," Sparks continued. "Everyone of us has different talents or gifts, but He takes all of us for His own work.

"There are no spiritual giants, dig it? The evangelizer is no closer to the Father than some poor little guy who is barely able to push a broom. Man, that's why it's so great."

"Amen."

The sermon was down-to-earth, but also essentially unemotional. Sparks's voice remained even and his appeal was being directed to intellects, not emotions.

After about twenty minutes, the Bible rap became a Scripture reading. Everyone in the room who had a Bible opened to Paul's letter to the Ephesians and began reading verses. First a person on one side of the room would read a verse, and then someone way over on the other side, then a person in the middle or sitting up on the stairs—all absolutely spontaneous. Not once did two people start reading at the same time. It was an incredible thing to watch.

After the readings, Sparks made an announcement. "Now is the time in this session that we pass the hat," he said. That seemed fair enough to me. Two hundred of us were sitting in his living room and a little donation certainly seemed in order, but this hat-passing had a certain twist to it.

"If you have any extra money, put it in," Sparks said. "If you need money, take it out. I don't expect to see any money in this hat when we're through passing it. Now let's bow our heads in prayer."

That was a new one to me. I bowed my head with the rest, but I couldn't keep myself from peeking at the passing hat. Some emptied their pockets into it. Some dropped bills into it. Some carefully counted certain amounts to remove from it. Others just grabbed out a bunch of bills and stuck them into their pockets. When the hat got to me, I dropped in two dollars and passed it to a guy on my left who promptly took them out.

While the hat was circulating and the heads were bowed, people would utter short prayers of thanksgiving out loud.

"Thank you, Father, for letting us call you Father."

"Thank you Lord for this fellowship, and we pray to you especially tonight for the people behind the Iron Curtain."

"We need a truck, dear Lord," Sparks said. "And we thank you now, because we know through your kindness we'll find a way to get one."

"Thank you, Lord, for sending me here tonight," a frail, brown-haired girl sitting behind me whispered. "I didn't know where I was going, but for the first time in my life, I feel as if I am home."

When the service was over, I talked to some of the young men in the room. Most of them were members of an organization called the Christian World Liberation Front, which was founded by Sparks and another layman, Pat Matrisciana.

Howard Criss, a bearded and barrel-chested Hawaiian, told me that a few years ago he used to spend his spare time heckling street preachers. "I was brought up a Roman Catholic, but I gave up on all religion pretty early.

"One day I was hitchhiking and a guy picked me up and said he'd like to share the Gospel with me. He was talking about stuff I had heard all my life but this time it really blew my mind. I really wanted to listen to him. Then he asked me if I wanted to receive Christ as my Lord and Savior, and I said no, not really. He said 'What do you have to lose,' and I said 'I guess nothing.' 'And what do you have to gain?' he said. 'Everything.'

"So pretty much as a favor to the guy, I said, 'Okay Christ, I want you as my Lord and Savior.' And inside, I was thinking, oh God, I wish this could be for real.

"But nothing happened.

"Then about a year later I moved in with some guys in Berkeley and one of the guys was a Catholic and he took me to the Newman Center and I took communion."

"Did you go to confession to a priest first?" I asked.

"I went to confession to the *high* priest," Criss said, smiling and pointing skyward. "But right after I took communion, I started crying out for God and I felt like He was there, taking care of me and loving me.

"That was over a year ago, and now I'm living here in the house, helping with the ministry, and learning just how to trust Him."

"And you know," he said with his rich baritone at an absolute matter of fact, "it gets easier all the time."

The fellow called Foxy, the one who had taken my two-dollar donation, seemed anxious to tell his story.

He had been a Weatherman, he said, and had been kicked out of the Army and at one time or another had been involved in just about every left-side-of-the-law activity he could think to name. "I've been involved in a lot of problems and I've tried a lot of solutions," he said. "But a right relationship with God provided by Jesus Christ is the only one I know that works."

Later I met a 25-year-old Puerto Rican named Hector who had been a member of New York City's revolutionary group, the Young Lords.

"When I was fourteen, I dropped out of the home scene and went to live on the Lower East Side where I became warlord of a street gang called the Barons. I spent three years just messing around, smoking some grass, popping some pills," he said in his earnest, slightly accented voice.

"Then I was in the Army for two years, got out, joined the Young Lords, and eventually came out here to get in on the dope traffic.

"I was on the campus one day and I heard this long-haired guy talking about Christ. But it was a real letdown. Nothing he said meant anything to me.

"But then someone introduced me to Pat Matrisciana and he invited me to lunch. Afterwards he asked me how I was fixed and I said I was broke so he gave me a couple of bucks.

"This sounds corny maybe, but it was the first time in my life anyone seemed to show any concern for me. It really got to me. He seemed so genuine and loving and together. I didn't know what this guy had, but I wanted it too.

"Right there in the restaurant, I leaned back and I felt this tremendous peace and joy come into my heart. It happened right there. A little later, I asked Christ into my life, and that's where I am right now."

Hector then began talking about organized religion and his Latin temper showed a little.

"The churches *fail*, man. They're either too much on spiritualism or too much on social action. Christ is the balance.

"Last year we went to the National Presbyterian Assembly in Rochester, New York," Hector said and it was obvious that whatever happened at that assembly was something he didn't like very much. "They had this vote, can you dig this? On whether to have prayer at the beginning and end of each session. And you know how the vote came out? No! They shouted no! And then they went and voted to give money to the Black Panthers and Angela Davis.

"Man, there's so much guilt and hypocrisy. They give

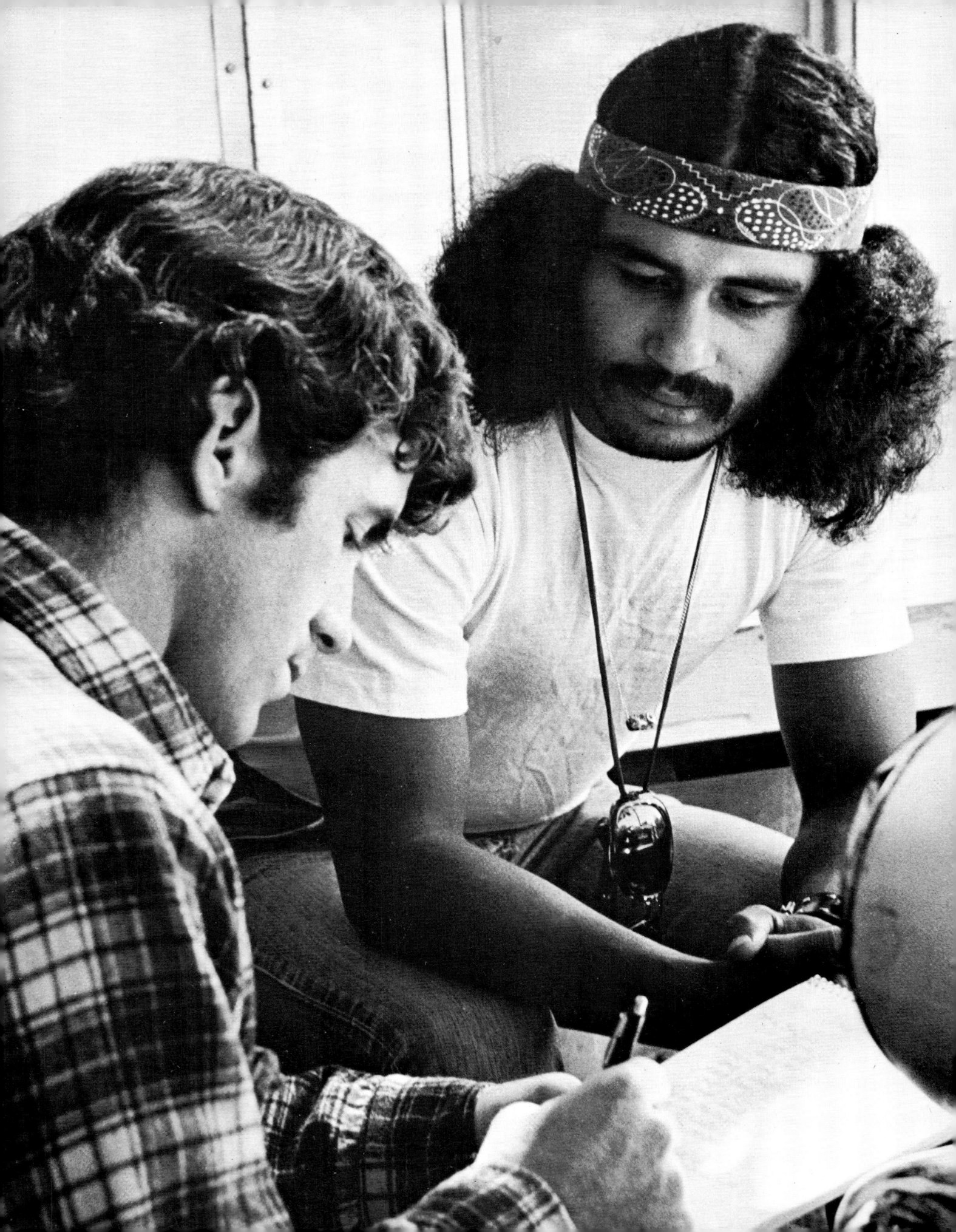

away that money but look at the pictures they paint of Jesus. Lily white. And blacks and Puerto Ricans can't identify with that stuff.

"Where did Jesus live, in the Middle East, right? And so he had olive-colored skin—skin colored like mine," Hector said with a touch of pride now taking over his voice. "And He was olive-colored for a very good reason. To unite the blacks and the whites. And He loves us all unconditionally. You. Me. Everyone."

According to Jack Sparks—all national publicity to the contrary—the Christians are the ones who recently have dominated the atmosphere of the University of California at Berkeley campus. Various groups championing various causes have set up their speakers' stands and handed out their leaflets, but none with the steady relentlessness of the Christian groups—"Christians for Christians," "The Christian Information Group," "The Christian World Liberation Front," and the especially zealous "Jews for Jesus."

If the Berkeley campus is the national hotbed of radical action, the testing ground for protest—the new Christians there have to know what they are doing. They have to be an elite fighting force, I would think, if they hope to win one convert in one thousand.

"We figured that if we could succeed in bringing people to Christ here, then we could succeed anywhere," a tall, full, radiant young woman named Susan told me.

She said she had been a Christian for five years and had watched the movement slowly materialize in the Berkeley area, evolve and mature and take root.

"At first we all wanted to go to the ghetto and make converts for Jesus," she said. "We'd go up to the first black guy walking down the street and say, 'Do you know the Lord?'

"Now what do you think that black is going to say to me, Miss Lily-white Blue Eyes from Bel Aire? We were so filled with zeal, but we were so stupid! We didn't have any idea about communication. We were so anxious to push Jesus, and we didn't begin to know how.

"I remember back in those early days in the commune where we lived together. We'd all be kneeling around praying for like an hour and we'd all be starving. You know, we hadn't eaten anything for hours and hours. But we'd be kneeling and kneeling—praying and praying. It was so dumb!

"But slowly we began to learn. We got off that guilt trip and our blind missionary trip. We began to organize. If the people in Berkeley were going to come to know Jesus Christ, we were going to have to raise a real ruckus to get them. And that's what we did."

The various Christian houses in Berkeley (there were over twenty when I was there) got organized. They began publishing a newspaper, distributing pamphlets, tracts, Jesus T-shirts, buttons, flyers, and most significantly, they virtually monopolized controversial Sproul Plaza—the free speech quadrangle fought for and won by the Berkeley radicals, circa 1960.

"The Jesus Freaks," as they were quickly dubbed by the campus, began to occupy the speaking steps of the Plaza two, three, and four times a week.

"Our kids meet informally to sing on Sproul Plaza day after day," Sparks says with obvious pride. "Then they sit around and talk to people—not badger or challenge them, just talk to them.

"The radical movement is still really at an explosive point here in Berkeley, but wherever it moves, our people have been in the midst. We have been in the middle, being God's people, showing love and concern that people need."

The Christians of Berkeley are almost conscientiously nonpolitical, though there are no stated bylaws or implicit instructions to keep them that way.

"Here, we just figured it would be best that we have no specific political enemies," one girl told me. "We have trouble enough as it is without choosing sides on some political issue. And how important is that issue going to be tomorrow anyway? Or the day after tomorrow?"

And so the Berkeley Christians have kept their beliefs and their evangelizing honed to a fine, intellectualized fundamentalism.

"What's your stand on the war?"

"As a Christian, I think war is generally wrong."

"What about the Crusades?"

"I have to be more concerned about what God's plan for tomorrow is than I am about what happened seven centuries ago."

"You mean you think going around talking about Jesus Christ has more relevance today than going around talking about atrocities that the industrial-military complex is committing all over the world?"

"I'd have to think that. Or else I'd have no reason for speaking at all. But look at it this way. If the majority of, say, just the college students in America talked about and practiced the teachings of Jesus Christ, do you think there could exist an industrial-military complex in America today?"

"They'd walk all over you."

"Maybe they would. I don't know. But they couldn't walk over the power of the word of God. It says here in the Bible that..."

"Oh come on. Don't pull that Bible crap on me. If you're going to talk religion, talk religion. But don't quote some musty old Scripture at me. I gave that up with Sunday school."

"Well I gave up Sunday school too. Probably at the same age you did. When did you quit?"

"I don't know. Ten... ten, eleven years old."

"Well I didn't smarten up until I was twelve."

"You mean you gave that crap up too!"

"Yea. I got sick of all that now-I-lay-me-down-to-sleep stuff."

"So what are you standing here preaching about Jesus Christ for?"

"Because Jesus Christ didn't say lie down and sleep. He said come, follow me. And he said whoever believed in him would have eternal life. That means anyone, any single person who believes in Jesus Christ as Son of God will never have to really die. Man, that's something to preach about."

"But you're talking from the Bible again. We're right back where you started. Quoting from something written two thousand years ago."

"Yes, I'm talking from the Bible again. I'm talking about God from the word of God. If I'm going to be pushing Jesus out here, I'd rather have God's words as my source material. Here you've got the author of the universe's only published work. I'd be pretty stupid quoting from anything else and ignoring this."

And on and on it goes. The Christian evangelists—whose appearance is pure campus camouflage: fatigue jackets, jeans, sandals, headbands—are getting exactly what they want. Recognition. Resistance. But mainly, participation.

Off to one side, a dozen Hare Krishna devotees—with their chalk-white, shaved heads, faded orange saris, and endless chanting—are virtually unnoticed by the regular

students. Only campus visitors stop and stare a while. But the Christians are working up a dialogue. The students aren't ignoring them, and that's what they want—to be noticed.

"People falling down on their knees and saying, 'Oh Jesus, yes! I accept you as my personal savior' is fine," said one young evangelist. "I can dig that. But it doesn't happen here very often. We don't go for the heart. We go for the head. If we can get people intellectually accepting Christ as son of God and savior of mankind, then the rest will take care of itself. But first we've got to break down the barriers that the traditional Christian churches have built up in these kids all their lives. That's why we stick with basics."

A survey conducted by the American Jewish Committee during the height of the Haight-Ashbury dominance over the country's youth culture showed that thirty percent of the hippie community was Jewish. For a country that has only approximately a three-percent Jewish population (about five and a half million in the latest census), the Haight figure says something pretty significant about young Jews and their desire to break away from traditional ties. They broke away in droves, and fully embraced the uncomplicated, nonritualized life style Haight Ashbury represented.

But when the Haight deteriorated from haven to dope-infested hellhole, the hippie population dispersed. Some fled to the mountains—literally picked up all the belongings they could carry and trudged off into the hills, the Santa Cruz and Diablo ranges which are now dotted with tiny communes. Others drifted back to Berkeley where that original search for Utopia all began.

And others—many others—made a complete political and spiritual about-face.

Martin "Moishe" Rosen looks about as much like he belongs in a Christian revival as Billy Graham would taking top billing in *Fiddler on the Roof*. If an anti-Semite were asked to draw a caricature of the typical Jewish businessman, he would draw Marty Rosen.

Marty is a heavyset, lumbering man with fleeting traces of New Yorkese in his conversation. What he does, I can't be so specific about. And neither can he, although whatever it is, he does it for about eighteen hours a day.

There is something in California called "Jews for

Jesus." It's not an organization, it doesn't have a membership or a central office or regular meeting place. Mostly, "Jews for Jesus" is a label put on all people who were born of the Jewish faith and who accept Jesus of Nazareth as their personal Messiah. If it is possible to be the unofficial, unelected, and unquestioned leader of a label, then that's what Martin "Moishe" Rosen is.

At one time, Mr. Rosen was something very specific. Having bucked and shocked an orthodox home early in life to embrace Christianity, he joined the American Board of Missions to the Jews in New York and with his Ph.D., efficiency, and quietly commanding presence, he became personnel director—number-two man of the whole outfit in charge of recruiting and training.

"I had impeccable credentials," he says with the sarcasm only vaguely veiled. "I had a book of letters from top clergymen all over the country telling me what a good job I had done in their churches.

"I had a large efficient staff who supported me magnificently. They knew what flight schedules I required and what accommodations I preferred. I was an organizational, structural dream.

"Then one day I was lecturing at a meeting of the Inter-Varsity Christian Fellowship at Columbia University. This was the kind of crowd I really knew how to win. I took a slam at hippies—borrowed a Ronald Reagan line. 'Hippies dress like Tarzan, walk like Jane, and smell like Cheeta. They say make love, not war, but they're capable of neither.'

"It brought the house down. It was that kind of crowd. But later a friend of mine came up to me and said, 'Did you ever smell a hippie?' I said 'Huh?' and he said it again. 'Did you ever smell a hippie?'

" 'No,' I said, setting up my defenses. 'I'd never get that close to one.'

" 'Well the next time you say someone smells, make sure you know what they smell like,' my friend said. I was cut down about as low as you can be cut.

"But then I started thinking. Thinking about people. I always sort of liked people. I went down to Greenwich Village and did a lot of listening—to hippies. And I liked what I heard. They seemed to be as open and honest as any segment of our society. Here I had been knocking the very people I should want to reach.

"Later I was invited to speak at the Golden Gate Seminary in San Francisco and what I saw out around there made my eyes pop. There were people—a lot of them hippies—and they were Christians and they were *active*. They were *doing* things."

The organization man had now completely lost his taste for organization. Rosen resigned his position with the Board of Missions and moved himself, his wife, and two daughters to Corte Madera in the San Francisco Bay area. Some of his former staff members thought he was crazy. Others resigned to come out and join him.

"I believe God wanted me to move here," Marty said matter-of-factly. "There are great needs in the Movement here. A lot of these kids have accepted Christ, but they need guidance. And there are a lot of Jews out here who need to find Christ."

Marty is essentially low-key, a cunning evangelizer with deceptive energy and a relentless determination that people come to accept Jesus.

"We had some Jews-for-Jesus posters made up and slapped about 250 of them around the Berkeley area. People would say 'what does that mean?' We'd say, 'we're Jews who are for Jesus.' They'd say, 'That's impossible. You can't be a Jew and a Christian at the same time. You have to be one or the other.' We'd say, 'That's nonsense. We couldn't possibly be anything else *but* both.' "

I got to meet a number of Jews who had accepted Jesus as their personal savior, and they seemed to be uniformly proud of their Jewish culture.

"We believe in the person of Jesus Christ as described in Scripture," 25-year-old Arnold Bernstein told me. "We say there is often a distinction between what Jesus taught and how the Christian churches interpret those teachings. My belief in Jesus is not a denial of my heritage but an affirmation of it."

The son of a Queens, New York, rabbi, Bernstein is now a part-time leather craftsman and a full-time evangelist in Berkeley. "There are a couple hundred of us Jews for Jesus here in the Bay area and we go around to rallies and meetings telling people how Christ saved and changed our lives. At first the reception was hostile but it's getting better all the time."

Ah ha! I thought I had uncovered an organization that Marty Rosen had pronounced did not exist. "What exactly is 'Jews for Jesus'?" I asked Bernstein.

He smiled pleasantly. "Oh, it's just a little fellowship that started about two thousand years ago."

I met other Jews who had embraced Christianity as their religion. In Anaheim, I was introduced to Don Abrams, twenty-two, who described himself as a "completed Jew."

At first as he spoke to me, he seemed wary—almost hostile.

"Yea, I came from a kosher home. And you want to know? I fell asleep at synagogue. I just couldn't stay awake."

As Abrams spoke, his wariness gave way to a kind of animated agitation—a show of energy that was a bit intimidating.

"I got to be where I was at the edge of an abyss, man. I was picked up by the shirt collar and held over the side of a cliff and looked down at hell. I was that far away from being at the bottom, man. Yea. Drugs.

"I needed help. I turned to Christ because I knew there was nothing in my own religion that could help me. I asked Christ into my life. Really *asked*. But nothing happened.

"Then I went through the ritual of water Baptism. That's supposed to really zing you. But for me there was no thunder and lightning—no horns sounding off in heaven."

Now the controlled surge of energy was almost at surface edge, ready to boil over. Abrams was talking faster.

"One day, man, I was working in a television shop, talking to a customer on the phone. I was saying, 'Yea, looks like you're going to need a few tubes and I got to fix a short in your transistor.' And then all of a sudden I said to the guy on the other end of the phone, 'Do you know that Jesus loves you?'

"And man, that's when it happened. At first, I was amazed. I just looked down at the phone—I couldn't believe I had said that. The guy, he just mumbled something about how he'd just have to fix the television himself. But something inside me started bubbling over—spreading all through me and outside of me."

And then Abrams' monologue came to its vociferous climax. He was describing to me what Christians call the Baptism of the Holy Spirit—something I would hear about many times in the months to come—but he didn't call it by name then. He just tried to describe what he said he knew was indescribable.

"I can't tell you, man, unless it's happened to you. There aren't any words. It's just this incredible feeling of God's love pouring through your body and gushing out all over. I haven't stopped talking about Jesus since that day."

I was told later that Abrams began a ministry specifically for "completed" Jews in a Los Angeles suburb.

Still another Jew I met who embraced Christianity was a young, handsome physician, Dr. David Sheiman who directed a Free Clinic in Long Beach. I met him at the Bethel Tabernacle in Redondo where he is one of the elders and referred to as simply "Dr. David."

I was introduced to Dr. David by Lyle Steenis, the pastor of Bethel. "Dr. David is a godsend," Steenis said. "He brings people in here every week, new converts to Jesus. And he's an amazing man. He speaks fluent English, French, Spanish, and Yiddish."

Dr. David, who had been looking at the floor in almost painful self-consciousness, suddenly looked up and smiled. "I speak a fifth language," he said. "I speak in tongues."

I asked Dr. David to tell me his story—where he had been, how he had come to know Christ, and where he was going.

"My story.... Well, I received my medical degree from the University of Mexico and then took several years of psychology. I worked in the New York mental health clinics and then returned to Mexico. I was getting divorced, I had emotional problems, I was flipping out, I had nowhere to go.

"I got into philosophy, sculpture, poetry, anything. I just kept looking for something to hold on to with both hands, and I couldn't find it. All that was in my head just wasn't doing me any good because in my heart I had fear and anxiety.

"Then one day, I read a book on the life of Jesus, and that spoke to my heart. It seemed to give me a warm feeling for the first time in my life.

"Even though I had been brought up in the Jewish faith, I decided after thinking about it that if there was really a God, then Jesus had to be His Son.

"Someone brought me here to this church, and I saw 150 people happy, singing and rejoicing. It wasn't like any religious service I'd ever seen. Something inside me kept telling me, Jesus is the truth. And so I said out loud, 'Jesus, if you are real, come into my heart.' At that moment I was filled with an indescribable joy—something I never came anywhere close to before. My life could never be the same again."

The first time I met Dr. David, he was running the Free Clinic all day with a very small staff treating hundreds of patients during the day. In the evenings, he would come often to Bethel for meetings and hours of prayer. He spent still more hours on the streets of Long Beach and Redondo—telling people how Jesus Christ had saved his life and urging people to accept the Lord.

When I returned to Bethel nearly a year later, on a Saturday afternoon, I found Dr. David on his knees—crouched before the huge wooden cross at the front of the church. His hands were raised into the air with the palms pointed outward and he was praying in the urgent, indistinguishable speech of tongues.

Then he looked up, saw the Cheethams and me, rose slowly to his feet and came over to us. He gave them each a crushing, cheerful bearhug, slapping Jack on the shoulder. "God bless you, friend. God bless you."

Then he shook my hand warmly and asked me what he had asked me the first time we met. "Have you accepted the Lord yet? You know there is no other way." I asked him what he had been up to for a year. "Oh, I've been running the clinic during the day and coming here to pray whenever I can," he said. "Then we spend time on the streets. There are thousands who have yet to come to know the Lord. And there isn't much time."

In just about every article that has been written about the Jesus Movement on the West Coast, the writer has visited Bethel Tabernacle. It is, along with being very spiritual, very good copy. Its congregation has the roughest backgrounds. They have the gut-true confessions to relate. Their spiritual rehabilitation is blatant, and their collective method of prayer to the uninitiated or the uninformed is downright bizarre.

The first time I went to Bethel, it was on a Saturday evening, and I was introduced to the church's pastor, Lyle Steenis. We talked in his small office above the church. His description fit his background: former lumberjack, boxer, jazz musician, and for the past twenty-five years, minister of the square, unadorned, and unaffiliated church in a middle-class suburb ten miles southwest of Los Angeles.

He told me the story of what had happened to his church in the last couple of years, and as he first told me, it was almost with a sense of bewilderment, as if he really didn't quite know what was happening.

"A young fellow came to me—he was nineteen then—Breck Stephens. And Breck said he thought he could start bringing young people into the church—the congregation at that time was all middle-aged or older.

"So I said go ahead. See what you can do. What he did was go down by the piers and get the junkies and speed freaks and get them into this pickup truck he had. He'd bring them into the church by the truckload—sometimes he actually would have to carry them. And they were a pretty scurvy lot. Some of them would nod off or pass out in the aisles, and the rest of the congregation was getting pretty upset.

"One night during prayer meeting, some of the adults got uptight and said we'd have to throw the kids out of the church. Well, I'm not a fighting man anymore, but I went down into the center aisle and said I'd whip any person who tried to run off any one of those kids.

"That was pretty much it for the adult congregation.

"But the kids kept coming. After a while, it got so they were telling other kids about the services and we were getting a packed house every night for prayer meeting.

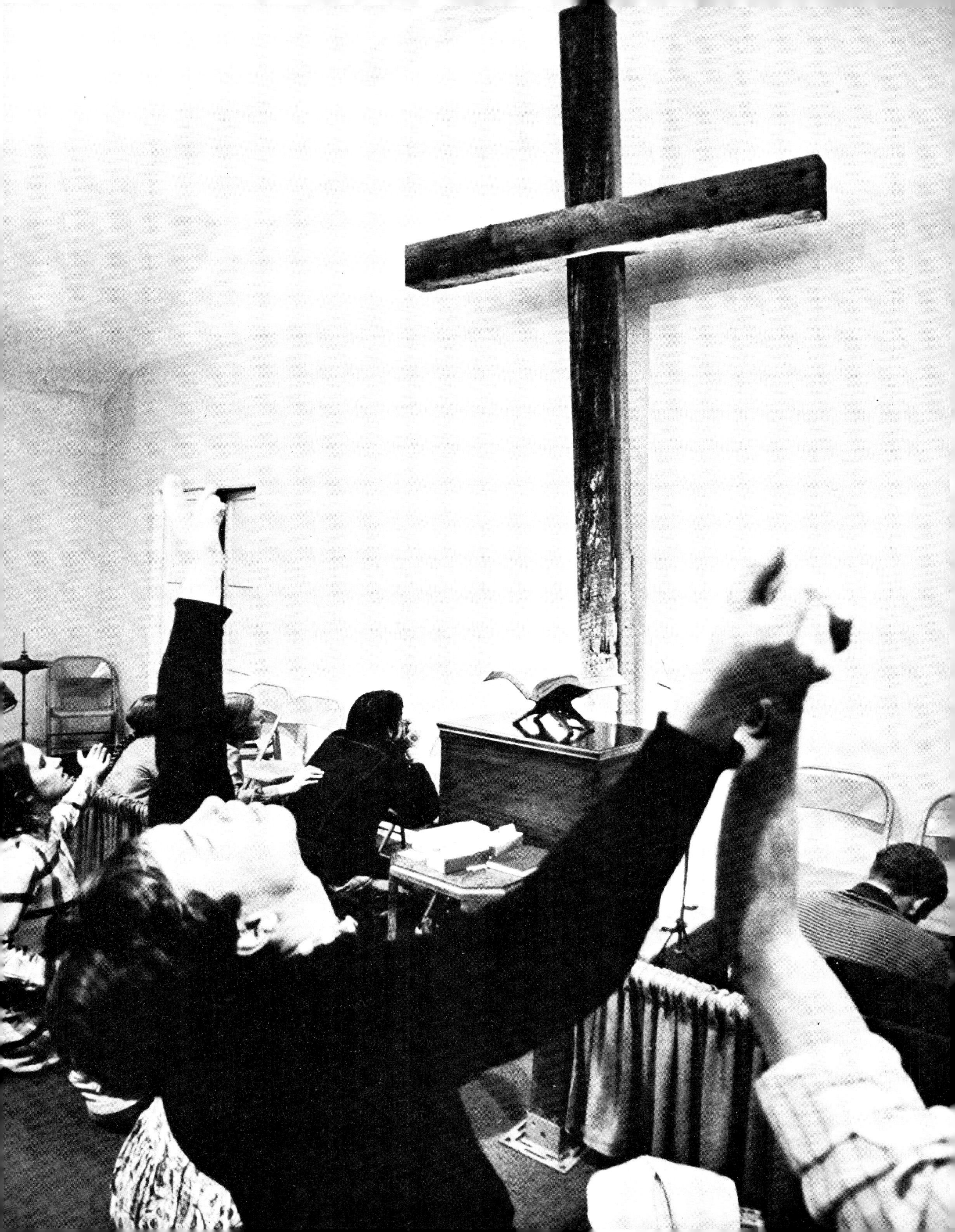

"For twenty-two years I had been praying for a revival, and this was it. But I made sure I stayed out of the mainstream. I turned it over to Breck. He conducts the services here, and it's been just fantastic."

While Pastor Steenis was talking, I was hearing that eerie sound coming from below the office. Loud unintelligible wailing, a kind of berserk begging sound rising up from the level below. It was the sound of human voices, I was pretty sure of that, but that was all I was sure of. I must have looked as worried as I was.

"That?" said Steenis. "They're speaking in tongues. One of the gifts of the Holy Spirit. Acts, Chapter 1, verse 8: 'But you shall receive power, after that the Holy Ghost is come upon you: and you shall be witness to me both in Jerusalem, and in all Judaea, and in Samaria, and unto the uttermost part of the earth.'

"God just takes hold of their tongues and lets them pray. They get filled with the Holy Spirit and those of them that are on dope go home and get healed and never go back to drugs again."

I left Steenis and went down to the prayer room where about fifty young people were letting the Holy Spirit do their talking for them. It was frightening but I couldn't take my eyes away. Fifty kids with their arms in the air, eyes half-closed, pained expressions on their faces, calling out their supposedly spirit-inspired litany of gibberish.

Then Steenis passed the word that the services were about to begin and with a kind of suddenness, the praying calmed to a halt and the crowd—a roughhewn lot—rose to their feet, smiled, and shook hands with each other, and entered the main body of the church.

Breck Stephens—the young licensed minister who turned Bethel into a Pentacostal haven for the young, mostly ex-heroin addicts—climbed up onto the short flat stage and walked over to the podium. He looked like what you would expect someone who single-handedly threw junkies into the back of a truck to look like: clean, with square-jawed good looks, and the body of a young steelworker.

Stephens began the service with song, and Pastor Steenis moved to the back of the church and manned a spangled set of drums. The music was loud and raucous and infectiously enthusiastic. They sang "Old Time Religion" and stomped around the church with an almost militant pace, clapping their hands and singing.

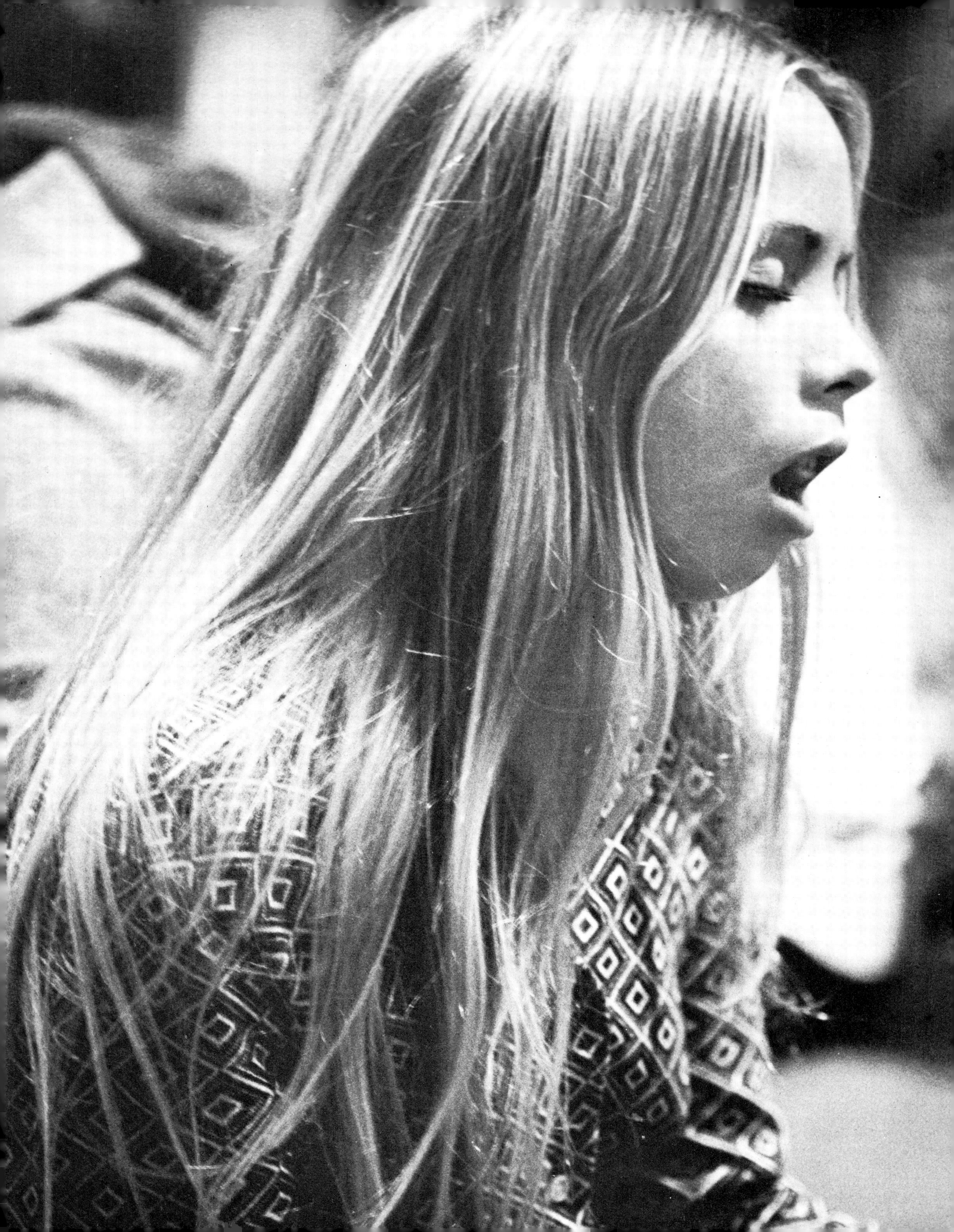

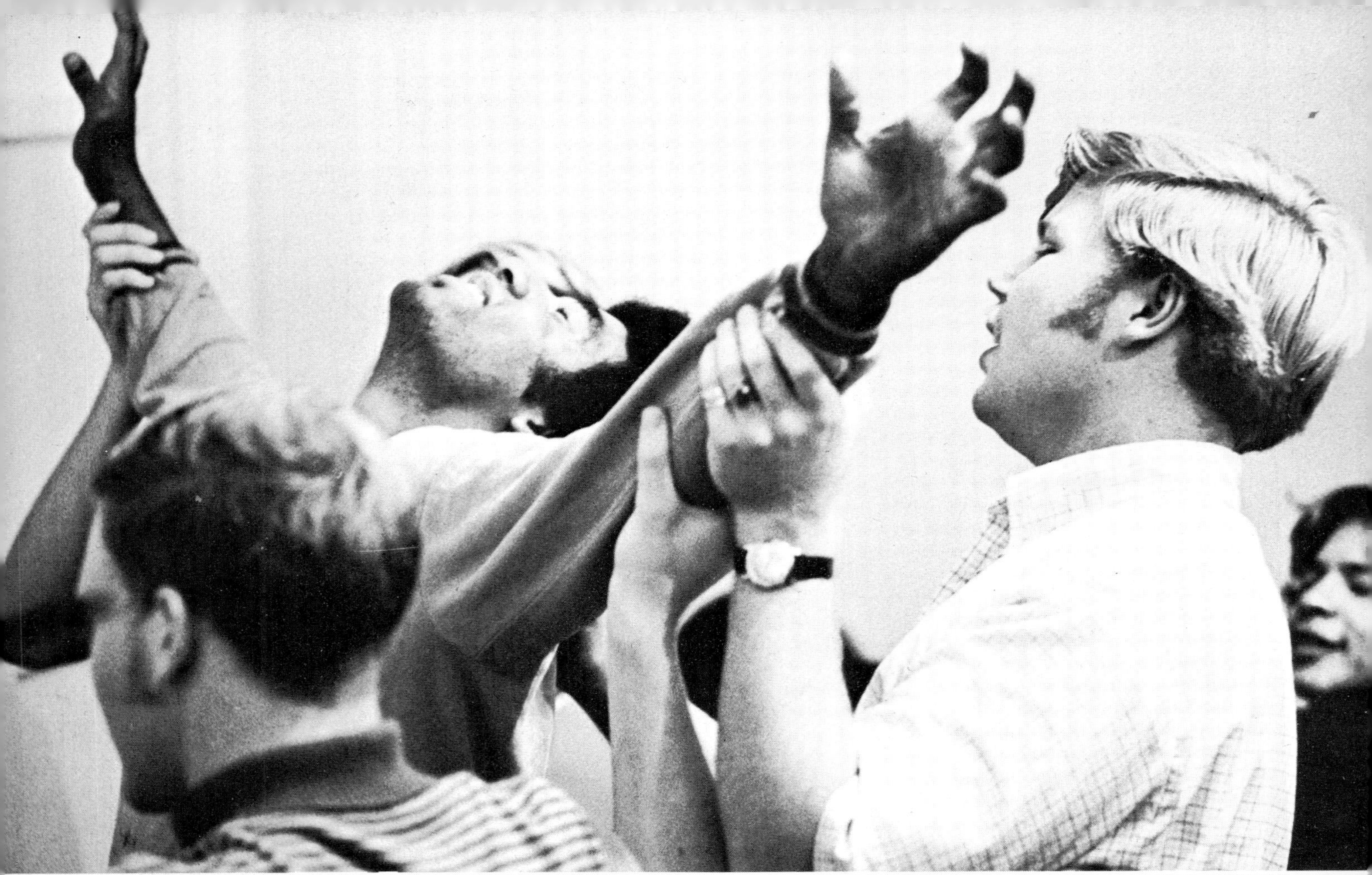
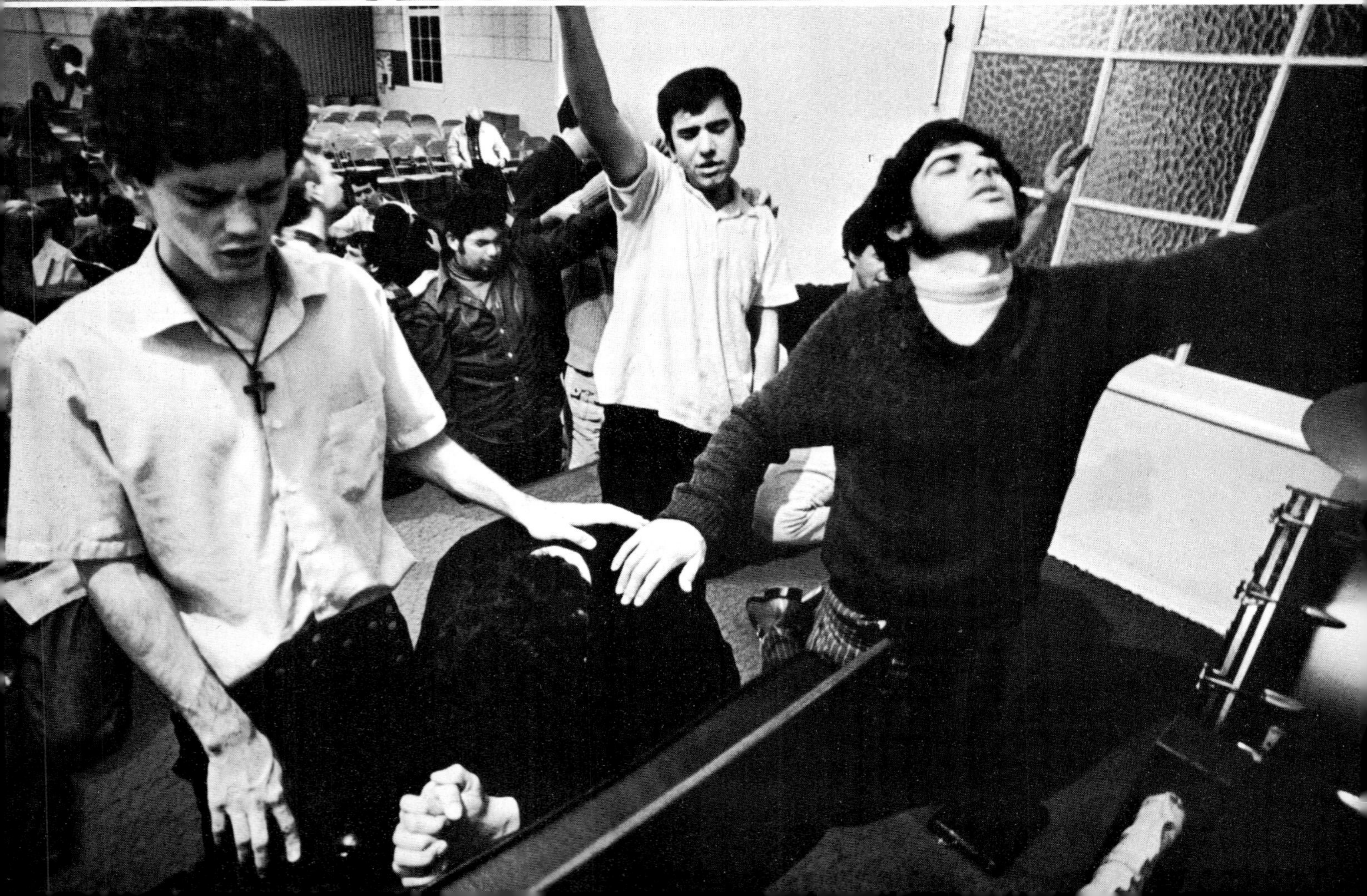

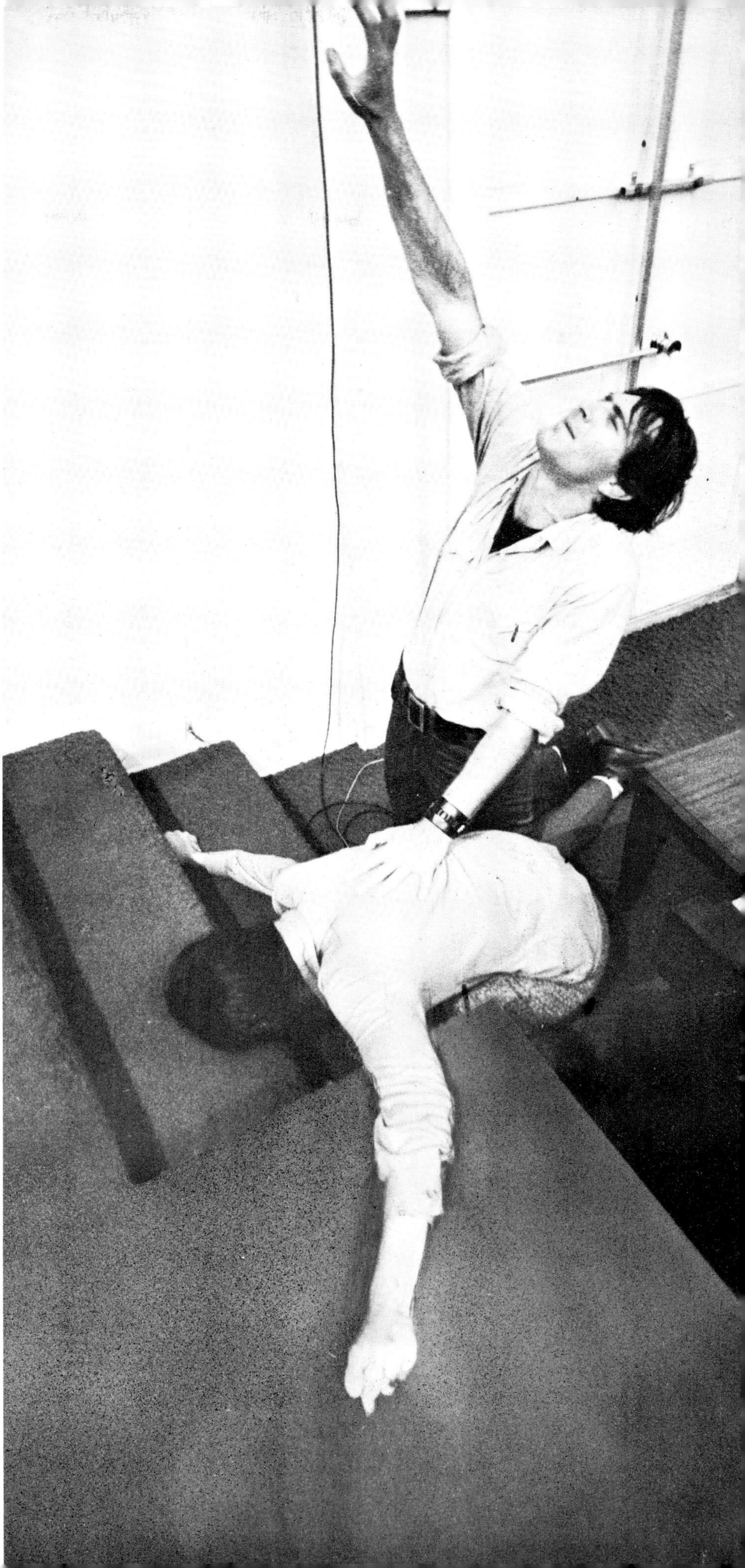

When the singing stopped, the congregation returned to their seats and the witnessing began. One by one, people would come up to the altar and tell their particular, grisly story of the life they led before they knew the Lord.

It was a procession of young people who had seen the ugly underbelly of this world far too early in life.

George and Kathy had been into black witchcraft, but when they came to Bethel they surrendered the tools of their craft on the altar—a leather bag filled with bones, a pentagram necklace, a spray they said had worked as an aphrodisiac, and several vials of potions.

"They told us anything we did was okay except things that had to do with Jesus," George told the congregation. They were smiling up at him, encouraging him. Some of them nodded in understanding, knowing where he had been.

Kathy came up to the podium timidly, ashamed, and described a black witchcraft ceremony in which she had volunteered to take part. "I had to put my hand on a Bible and say: 'I will never, ever read this book again.'" Faltering, she went on. "I went home that night and I saw that my hand was becoming discolored and sore. The next morning my whole arm was abcessed. I knew then that what I had done was awful wrong. I knew I had done something to offend God. I knew I had to come back to Christ."

"Amen," the congregation said.

Sixteen-year-old Paul came up to the lectern. "My folks used to strap drugs onto my body and put me on an airplane. They used me as a carrier back and forth across the country. When I complained, they let me shoot up too, to make the trips easier. Pretty soon, I was an addict.

"Finally, at the Los Angeles airport, I got arrested for interstate transportation of drugs. I had to be in the infirmary for two weeks for withdrawal and then I was put in Juvenile Hall. But I escaped, and started shooting up again.

"Finally, for no special reason, I started living with some people who had been saved. I just needed a place to stay, but they got to talking to me. They said if I asked Jesus into my heart, I wouldn't have to go through withdrawal again. I did, I asked Jesus to help me, and they were right.

"But when I first started coming here and seeing everyone speaking in tongues, I thought it was some kind of psychological trip," Paul said. The congregation nodded knowingly.

"I thought it was just a lot of bull. But then I found out it wasn't. I found out I could do it too. Jesus loves us all so much, he even lets *me* pray in tongues."

Charles, a baby-faced, blond, bearded giant came to the podium. "I was never really that much into drugs, but I had my own worldly hell. I was getting involved in physical love orgies. The devil was inside me, and all the time I had to have sex.

"Then I started living with my girl friend. But I could hear Jesus in my heart, telling me I had to straighten myself out. And I knew I couldn't be living in sin and receive the Holy Ghost. So I moved out of my apartment and moved in with my parents. At first it was a problem because I was a Christian and they weren't. And of course my girl friend was mad at me. But I worked at it, and prayed, and then my girl got saved and now it's beautiful."

"All right!" the congregation shouted enthusiastically.

Joe, a twenty-year-old Chicano, came to speak. "I was on drugs for nine years when Breck brought me here. I didn't know where I was going or anything. I was all freaked out. But I started praying when I got here, and I just got cured. They say the mercy of God endures forever. Man I tell you, He sure had mercy on me.

It was sixteen-year-old Leslie's turn to talk. "I started taking reds when I was thirteen. Up until a few months ago, I was using ten a day. But then one day, I was just hit with the thought that Jesus died for me, and that he must care for me. I threw all my dope into the ocean.

"If there are any of you out there who don't know him yet, you really ought to try it. I know it seems a far out thing to say you know Jesus personally. But I really don't know anyone in the world as personally as I know Jesus."

"Amen!" the congregation shouted.

Then a thin blonde girl, twisted and spastic, was led onto the stage by an older girl who explained they were sisters. "This is Diane, and when she was born, she was deaf, dumb, and almost totally paralyzed. The doctors told us she would never be able to even walk.

"But we prayed for her and taught her to pray, and she has made progress that has absolutely astounded the doctors." Then Diane began speaking to her older sister enthusiastically in the language of hands, her face contorting into a grin.

"She says," her sister translated, "that next year she will be able to talk like us."

"Oh praise God," the congregation shouted. A real

feeling of excitement was mounting. I could sense the building feeling of joy and ecstasy in the room. It was something I could feel in my stomach and almost grab with my hands.

It was then time for a guy named, appropriately it seemed, Mike Dragon to come to the stage. He was older than most of the people in the room—maybe thirty-five—and the toughest looking of all. I was told he had spent twenty years pretty heavily involved in drugs, and that at one time he had been a Hell's Angel. I didn't need any convincing. He looked the part, and that's what made his words—spoken slowly and gently—seem all the more incongruous.

"Lots of times in my life I got to thinking, now is the only reality. What is happening at this moment is the only thing of importance. There is nothing else, only this moment.

"I used to think that a lot, and it wasn't a very good thought. Then one day I just somehow realized how wretched I was. And I found Jesus . . . No. Jesus found me. And he filled me with the Holy Spirit. And now I know there is eternal life. With him."

When the testimonies were over, Breck Stephens took over the stage. When I had first been introduced to him, he seemed shy and even a little backward. But up at the lectern before his congregation, he was a vibrant dynamo—occasionally pounding the lectern to emphasize a point, walking up and down the stage, speaking with unquestionable authority.

"We used to be hippies, didn't we? We used to be love children. We loved everyone, didn't we?

"Sure we loved everyone. Except the police. And our parents. And anyone who wanted to take our dope away from us.

"Now we really do love everyone."

"Amen!"

"Because we know we are all brothers and sisters in Christ, and we know the Bible teaches us to even love our enemies.

"I know it's not easy sometimes—it's easy to get ticked off at people. I used to work in a restaurant and the owner gave me such a hard time I really wanted to let him have it. But I had my Bible with me, and I'd just touch it, and remind myself of what it teaches, and I'd love the guy."

Breck's sermon was direct and down to earth. He talked mostly about love, and the need for love on earth and love for God. At the end, his message seemed to be very specifically pointed.

"We're not trying to outdo anyone out here. We're not saying that Bethel is the best place that God works, or that we are special in the eyes of God.

"We're just trying to help each other. We're not trying to outpray or outsave or outshout one another. We need to encourage each other. We need to work together to praise the Lord and pass on his message to everyone. God's love is infinite. We just have to join with other Christians everywhere and tell people about it."

When I returned to Bethel after a year, I had to wonder if Breck had changed. He had been photographed for half a dozen magazines, appeared on a television talk show and some radio interviews. Could he still feel he wasn't just a little bit special? Could he still be that dynamic and yet that humble?

When I walked into Bethel that Saturday afternoon and greeted Dr. David, I saw many of those grim ex-addicts praying in tongues. It was about three in the afternoon, and I was told some of them had been there since early that morning. Breck was kneeling on the floor with his head bent over the pew seat in front of him, his words mouthed silently. Others were praying loudly, in tongues, hands in air, while still others were sitting with their backs against the wall, looking straight ahead with glazed expressions in their eyes, Bibles in their laps.

Then suddenly—almost on cue, though nothing particular triggered the event—the praying stopped and people began to stir. Young men and women, mostly in their teens, began to stand up, blinking as if they were suddenly struck with sunlight, or as if they had been asleep. And they looked pleased—as if that sleep had been a pleasant one. They stretched and yawned, and shook hands with each other, greeting with the standard: "God bless you. God bless you, brother."

Something was happening and I couldn't figure out what it was. Moments before, the small, stark church sanctuary had been alive with the wailing sounds of the Pentacostals—fifty or more kids in loud, solitary prayer. And now all of a sudden the church seemed like the camp of a small army at dawn, slowly waking up to meet a new day.

It turned out my simile wasn't a bad one. Breck spotted

me and came over to give me that handshake you always remember for about an hour later. "Bless you, brother," he said. I asked him what was happening, and he said the people in the church were getting ready to go down to the waterfront and give witness. It was indeed an army meeting a new day, an army mobilizing for an assault on non-Christians.

I drove down to the waterfront with Breck and asked him what the year had been like. "Your article in *Look* was certainly a blessing for us." he said. I didn't know whether to say "thank you" or "think nothing of it" or what.

"A lot of ministers and priests came to the church after the article to see if we were for real. They only have to come once and they're convinced."

"You've been pretty much in the limelight youself," I said. I almost felt like apologizing for helping to put him there.

"I'm just working for the Lord," he said simply. "I'll do whatever he wants me to do."

Breck Stephens hadn't changed.

Bethel Tabernacle, however, had. Pastor Steenis told me that since the publicity had been given to the little church, people were coming by the thousands.

"A few years ago, we'd have a Sunday morning adult worship service and maybe one prayer meeting a week," Steenis said. "When Breck came and the adult congregation left, we expanded to three prayer meetings a week.

"Now the church is just a constant prayer meeting. It's open twenty-four hours a day, and I don't think you can come in here any hour day or night that there aren't a few praying and having fellowship.

"We started this program three years ago, and I'd say 60,000 kids have come here one time or more since we began. Then they go on, go home or whatever, and start up their own movement in Christ. It's spreading so wild, it's unbelievable.

"Ministers come up to me and they want to know what my program is. I say I don't have a program. In fact I try to stay out of the mainstream as much as possible, to keep from polluting it.

"But they say, come on, tell us, what's the secret. And I just say these kids come and get filled with the Holy Spirit and that's all. They won't believe me until they see it happen."

When Breck and I got down to the waterfront—a tourist attraction of Redondo called Fisherman's Wharf—I asked

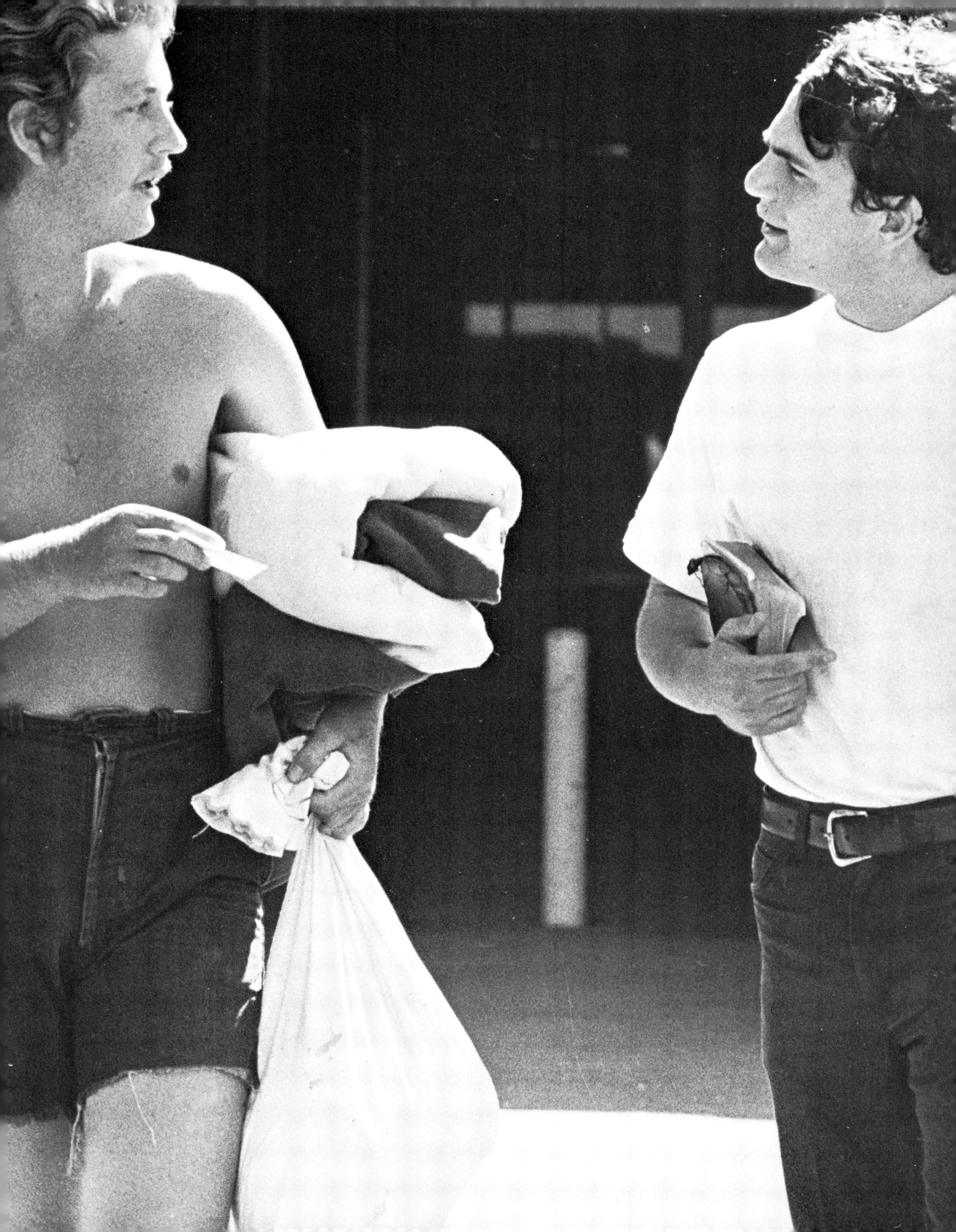

if I could just hang around for a while and see how things went. He said sure.

Breck and a tall, bearded fellow formed one team, walking up and down the boardwalk, stopping anyone, with the abandon of street beggars, with a question that came right to the point.

"Say, would you like to know Jesus?"

"Not really," one tanned surfer said as he tried to walk away from the two young ministers.

"Hell's going to be a horrible place to spend eternity, you know," Breck said.

"I live for today, not for tomorrow," the surfer said, still walking.

But Breck was being persistent. "How about living for your soul?" he asked.

"I don't know that I have a soul," the surfer said.

"The Bible says you do, brother. Here, take this card." Breck handed him a small card with the address of Bethel Tabernacle and a schedule of formal services.

The surfer stuffed it in a pocket of his bathing suit and beat a hasty retreat.

Other members of the Bethel congregation had fanned out all over the boardwalk, stopping people their own age and getting right to the point. Some listened politely and others listened uncomfortably, keeping their eyes away from the young preachers, obviously stuck in a situation they didn't like and didn't know how to get out of.

Still others were argumentative.

"What do you mean 'God provides'?" one young man said angrily to Breck. "What about all the poor people in the ghettos? They're supposed to be religious and everything. What's God doing for them?"

"If they are religious, if they truly believe in Jesus Christ, then God is providing for all their needs," Breck said.

"That's a lot of crap."

"Well you might think so, but it says right here..." and Breck began to open his Bible.

"Hey, don't pull that out on me," the man said, backing away as if he were being forced to confront something totally hideous. "Don't give me that Bible stuff. We'll be standing here 'til the bars close."

Breck handed him a card. "We'd like to see you in church, brother."

"Yea, yea," the man said, now almost running backward.

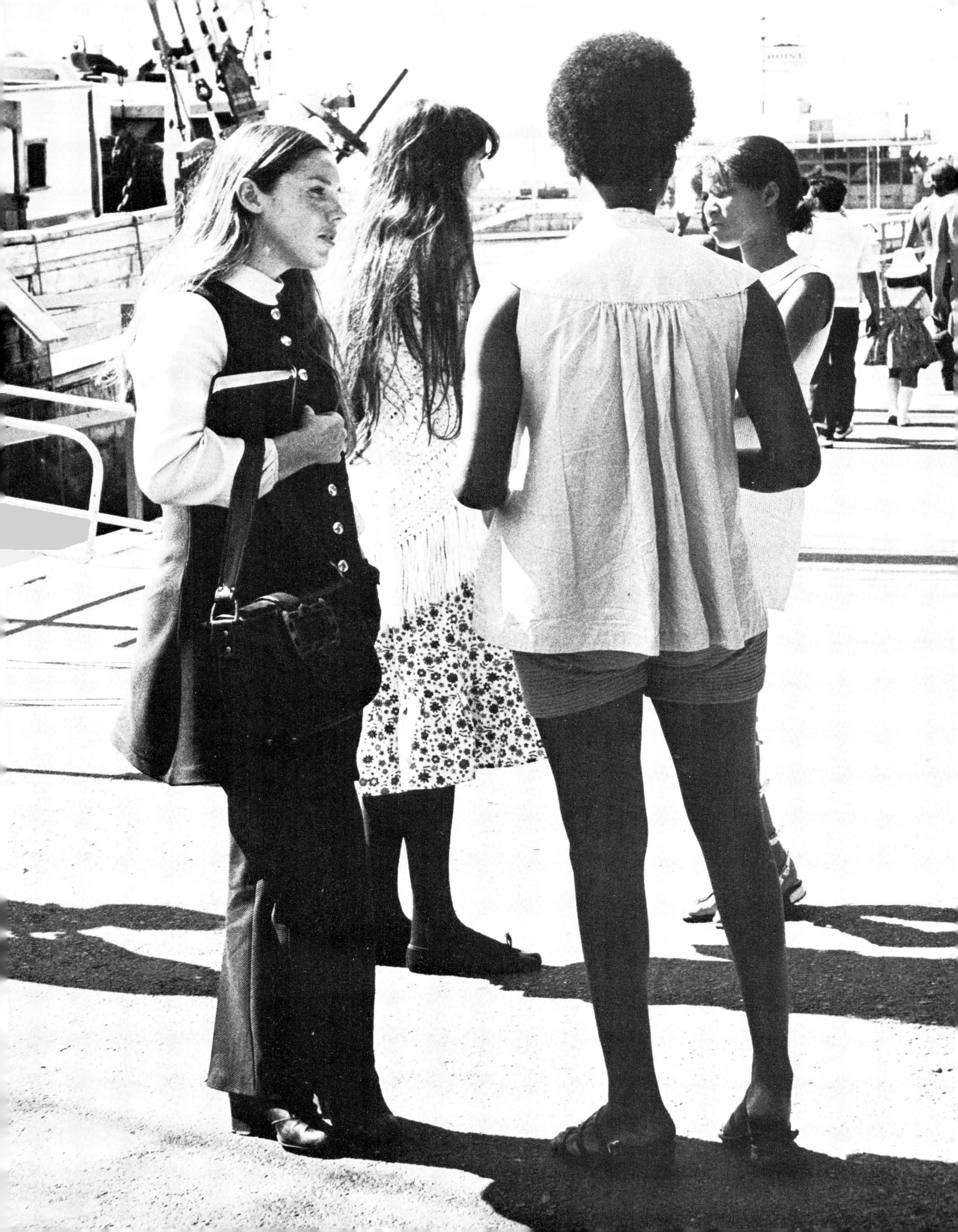

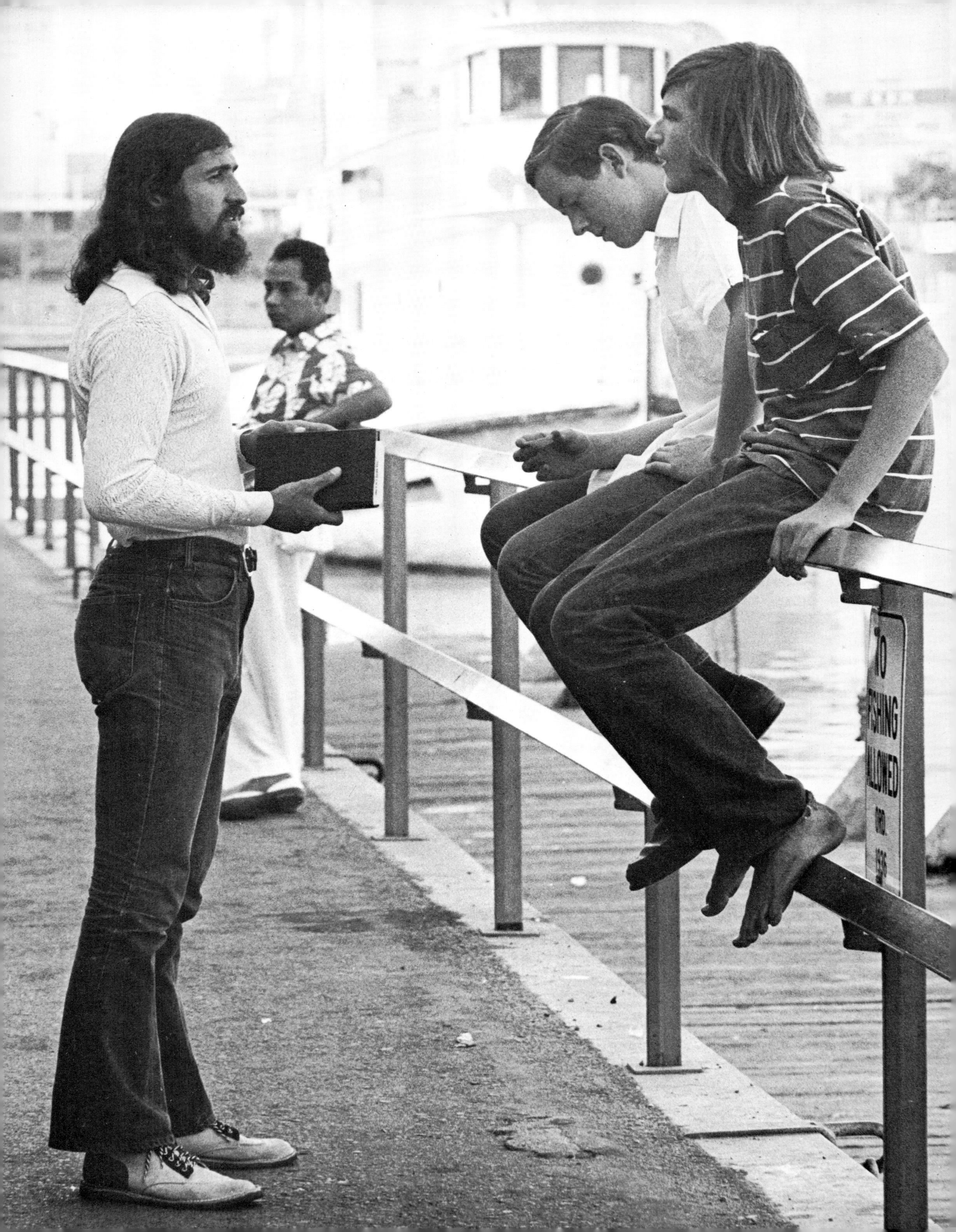
ALLOWED
ORD.

When he was out of sight, Breck turned to me and shook my hand—hard again. "See that?" he said excitedly. "That's the kind we usually get. He's the kind who's going to start wondering, 'What was I so scared about?' And then he's going to say, 'I wonder what that church is all about?' And he'll come down some night and we'll have him."

At first I thought Breck was acting like a college coach recruiting promising high-school athletes. And then I realized that's exactly what he was doing. Recruiting. That's what the whole gang of them was doing.

"Those guys, they're creeps," a lady proprietor of a gift shop on the wharf said to no one in particular, pointing to Breck and his partner who were witnessing to some girls twenty feet from her storefront. "I was saved fifteen years ago. That doesn't mean I have to go around telling everyone they're sinners, that they're going to go to hell.

"And I've been to their church, too. Gobble, gobble, gobble. . . ." The woman did a rather bad imitation of praying in tongues. "You talk about your weird Holy Rollers. That's them all right."

I went up to a young kid—he looked like he was about fifteen—who had just listened to one of the street ministers for about five minutes.

"What do you think of them?" I asked.

"Well I don't think they're nuts, if that's what you're asking," he said. "I just think they're very religious. But I wish they wouldn't come up to me so much. They stop me every time I come down here with that same stuff."

"Well why don't you just walk away from them," I said.

"I don't want to be impolite, I guess."

Nice kid.

Later, I talked to the young ministers about what they were doing. "Don't you guys ever get discouraged? I mean, you've been doing this several times a week for how long? Two years? And how many people will say, yes, they'll give themselves to Jesus. Out of the hundreds of people you talk to, how many times do you get through? How many people accept what you're saying?"

"Eight, this afternoon," someone said.

"Really?" Breck said as his face lit up. "Praise *God!*"

"Okay, eight today," I said, and I was impressed. "But still, I saw all the ones who said no—the people who walked away from you."

"One time I was coming off an LSD trip," Breck said to me, "and some guy came over and said something about accepting Jesus as my savior. I don't even remember what he said. But he planted a seed. That's what we're doing. Planting seeds. There's nothing discouraging about that."

Anaheim, California, is the home of Knott's Berry Farm and the convention center and Disneyland and an astonishing number of young people who call the Jesus Movement their own. The physical center of the activity is Melodyland, where Pastor Wilkerson conducts the adult services, and young kids by the hundreds are witnessing to young kids by the thousands all over southern California.

The three-pronged youth ministry includes a Speakers' Bureau—where new evangelists visit various schools and assemblies and give their own personal testimony—a touring choir called "The Chromatics" and a 24-hour "Hotline." It is probably this constantly available telephone service through which most Anaheim young people are given their introduction to Jesus Christ.

The Hotline office is located in one of the Melodyland wings, and is manned every hour of the night and day by youthful volunteers. The Hotline number is a simple one —778-1000—and young people are invited to call with any kind of problem they possibly have. They'll get advice— usually from someone who at one time experienced an identical problem—and then a little friendly evangelizing. The volunteers are Christians, and when someone calls up with a drug problem, an unwanted pregnancy, or even an announcement of suicide, they get advice and prayer and then a suggested section of Scripture to read.

"Hotline, may I help you?" says the young man. It's a little after midnight and before the phone rang, he had been sitting in an office chair, feet propped up on the desk, reading his Bible.

"Man, I'm in trouble," said another youth on the other end of the phone. "I can't get off my trip, man, and I'm really on a downer. I really need help!" The voice is desperation—total fear.

"Well, the first thing you have to do is calm down a little," the volunteer says.

"I've been taking reds, man. And they're not doing it. They're not doing anything! It's really a bummer, man. Can you help me? I mean you advertise that you can help people."

"All right, first tell me your name and where you are."

The young man on the other end of the phone says he is at a friend's house.

"Is your friend there with you?"

"No. I'm alone. And I'm scared!"

"Is your friend coming back?"

"I don't know."

"Do you have a way to get home?"

"No, man. Pete took the car. He's my friend. I mean I think he's my friend. He's Pete, you know? And he took the car."

"All right. Tell me where you live."

The young man gives his name and address.

"Are your parents at home?"

"Yea, my Mom is. But you can't tell my Mom I'm tripping. Man, what kind of rip off is this? What are you guys going to do? I need help."

"Right," the volunteer says, his voice soothing and even. "You're on a bad trip and you want to come down. And I'm going to help you come down. Then I'm going to call your Mom and tell her where she can come and pick you up. I'll say you got stranded and you need a lift."

"Yea, okay, but you got to help me now!"

"Okay, easy, easy. You're not the first person to ever get on a bad trip, you know. It's not the end of the world. Do you have a Bible with you?"

"A what?"

"Forget it. Have you tried praying?"

"Man, I can't pray. What are you trying to give me? What are you pulling on me?" The voice on the other end of the telephone is getting angry—less desperate. The volunteer at the Hotline office swings his feet off the desk and leans over it with his elbows. His voice is beginning to mean business.

"You called for help, right? Well there is someone you can ask for help right there where you are. And that's God."

"Man, I can't pray," voice now decreasing to a whine.

"Why not? Have you tried it?"

"God's not going to listen to me."

"Why not? Does God have something special against you? Doesn't the Bible say Christ, the Son of God, died for all men, for all their sins?"

"Yea. I guess so. I don't know. I'm on dope and everything."

"Try praying. God will listen. He's waiting for you to ask for His help. All He wants you to do is ask."

"What do I say?"

"Whatever is in your heart."

". . . Well God, here I am. And I hope You're up there and I hope You're listening to me because I really need Your help."

"He's listening to you."

"I really went and screwed up, You know God? I mixed speed in with my acid and I really screwed myself up. And I really don't know where to turn, You know God? I mean, if You could help me, I'd really appreciate it. I know I've sinned a lot and stuff, but if You could just forgive me this one time, man, I'd really be grateful. . . . Amen."

Then the volunteer began to pray. "Dear Lord, we ask you to help our brother. He knows he has done something against your will and he confesses that sin, knowing that you, in your great mercy, have already forgiven him. We ask that You stay with this brother, dear God, and give him the strength to walk always from now on according to Your law. We ask in Jesus' name. Amen."

There was silence for a moment, and then the volunteer said, "How do you feel now?"

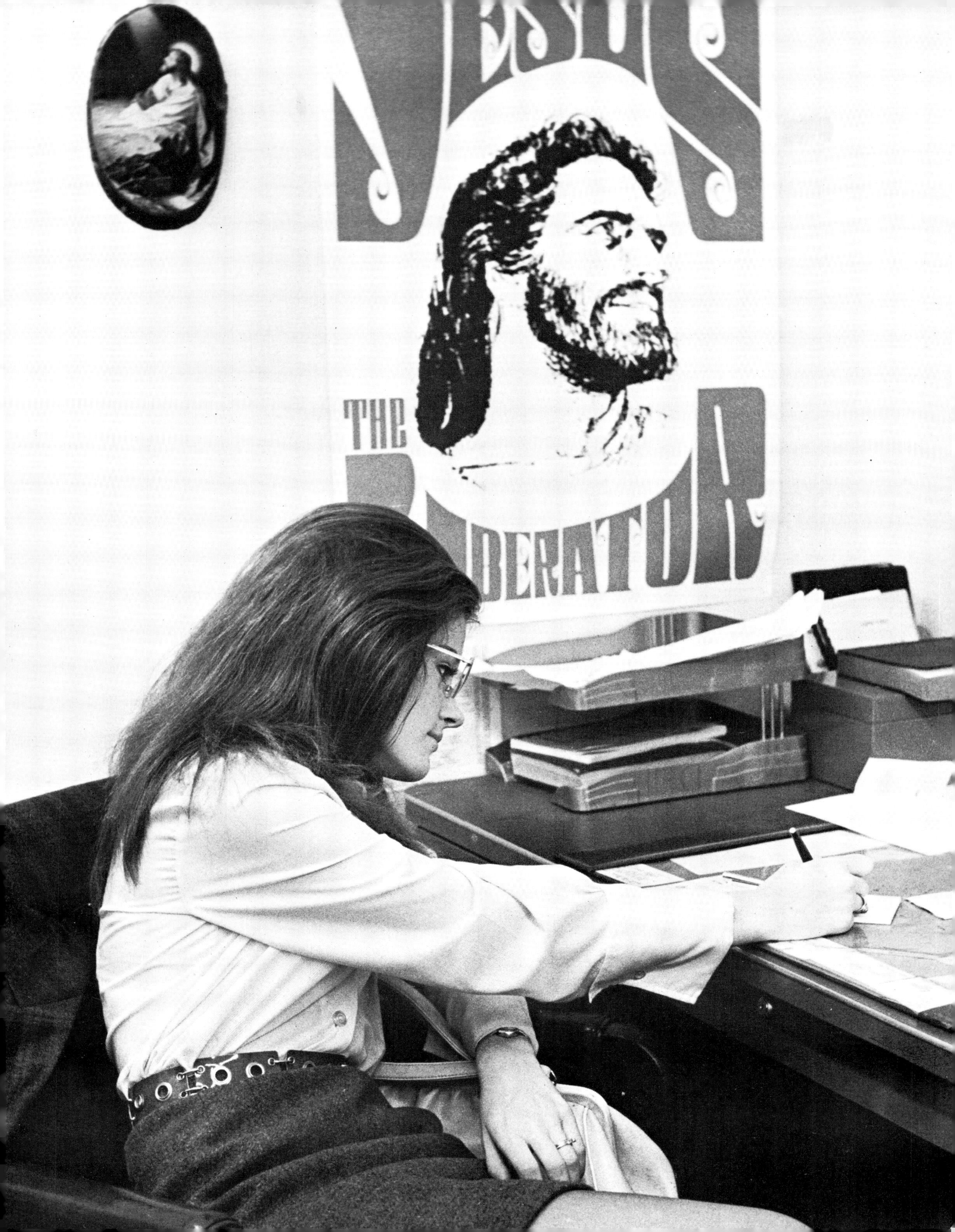

"I don't know. Better I guess."

"You feel like you're still tripping?"

"No."

"So it turns out God cares about you after all maybe."

"Yea. I guess so." The caller's voice is subdued, slightly bewildered. He sounds a little surprised—probably surprised more than anything by the fact that he prayed out loud, maybe for the first time in his life.

"Now I'm going to give your mother a call and . . . No, better yet, you call her. Tell her you're stranded and need a lift home. Will you do that?"

"Yea. I will."

"Good. And while you're waiting for her to come, try praying some more. You might even thank God for taking care of you."

"Okay."

"And you might also drop by here at Melodyland next Tuesday night. Every Tuesday we have a Hotline hour and you might like to come. Okay?"

"Yea. Okay."

"Good. And anything else we can do for you, feel free to call back. But you sound like you're in good shape now. God bless you."

"Yea . . . hey man?"

"Yea?"

"Thanks."

"Praise the Lord, brother."

Hotline strikes again. It started out with a handful of volunteers who often prayed that people would call to ask for help. Now they have sixty volunteers, average over 3,000 calls a month, and have a thorough system of follow-ups, mailings, and referrals to agencies of outside assistance. When necessary, the young volunteers contact Christian psychiatrists and doctors to lend a hand.

And the service is contagious, spreading throughout the country. The Anaheim Hotline Center alone has helped set up more than a dozen similar 24-hour Christian emergency lifelines. And they in turn have helped establish still more.

The director of the Melodyland Drug Prevention Center is George Wakeling, a down-to-earth, easygoing head counselor to the Hotline volunteers and to the hundreds of new young Christians in the area. He was not always so easygoing.

"A few years ago, he was kind of hard to live with," said his seventeen-year-old daughter Leslie, a girl one would call plump, pleasantly, infectiously exuberant and lovely. "He ran a drugstore, and at night he'd come home and be grouchy and yell at us kids. It wasn't much fun. He was getting ulcers.

"But we loved him anyway, and Mom prayed for him every day, and then one day he just got saved."

"You were making good money," I once said to George—not to bait him, but really to get some understanding. "You had a big house and a swimming pool and an expensive car. And your daughter says you were kind of lousy to live with."

"I was."

"And now you've got not such an expensive car, and a low salary, and no swimming pool, and a job that keeps you up to all hours at night, and a house with not only your own kids but half a dozen others that you've taken in, and you seem like a very happy man."

"I am. I'm satisfied with my life. I know what I believe in. And I know that if I were to die right at this very instant, I'd go to heaven. That's something to be pretty happy about."

"I guess so," I said.

It was people like George Wakeling who were most perplexing to me as I explored the Jesus Movement. If I asked enough psychologists, I'm sure I could get a clinical explanation for young drug addicts experiencing an instant cure, merely by calling out for the help of a deity. And I could see how hundreds and thousands of kids who were strung out on drugs and searching for some kind of peace of mind could embrace this fundamentalist Christianity with open arms because this was a guarantee of eternal peace, and for that matter, a very pleasant immortality. And I could see how young students who had delved into all kinds of Eastern and Western mysticism and religion could be caught up in the Christian revival. Because here was a religion where you were *loved* by your God. He sent His Son to die for your sins, so you've already been forgiven, even for stuff you haven't done yet. That's a pretty attractive deal. I could see some student after spending month after month trying to figure out how he came about and where he was going, taking Christianity and saying "Okay, this one's for me."

But George Wakeling. Kind of an average, early middle-aged, successful businessman—totally articulate and intelligent—to give up every aspect of his earlier life and center his new one around God and Jesus Christ. That's the kind of guy that I really wanted most to understand. That was the kind of guy I couldn't figure.

There is another one at the Melodyland Drug Prevention Center. Steve Kosca, a big swarthy ex-sheriff's deputy who quit the force to become George Wakeling's assistant. And his job has no salary.

"There was an opportunity a few months back where they could have worked out a way to put me on salary," Steve said to me. "But my wife Charla and I prayed to the Lord about it for a while and we decided to say no—we didn't need it.

"It's funny, but when we need money, it's always somehow there. We never go without the things we need. I remember one month, it got up to the thirteenth and we hadn't the money to pay the rent yet.

"The fifteenth came and went, and still there was no money."

I was thinking, here is one of those stories again. I mean I *know* it's going to end with Steve getting the rent money. I know there's going to be some kind of mini-miracle that makes everything turn out right at the last minute. But again, I find myself fascinated. Here's Steve Kosca. An ex-cop. Obviously bright and alert and not even remotely spaced out—on religion or anything else. But he's going to tell me a story about getting the rent money, a tiny bit miraculously, and he's going to look me straight in the face and tell me the Lord helped him get it.

"Finally, it got to be the seventeenth of the month and I decided I had to pay the rent. I didn't have a penny in the bank, but I wrote out a check for two hundred dollars and gave it to my landlord."

"You were bouncing a check. That's a little dangerous," I said, playing Steve's straight man.

"That's what my wife told me. Only she told me I was crazy. But I told her not to worry, that I just felt confident everything would turn out okay.

"Well that afternoon, some donations came in—a little here and a little there—but I was still a hundred dollars short. The next day was Friday, and I had to get that rent money into the bank before it closed.

"I had less than an hour to go and I walked into my office and there was a white envelope on my desk. And inside was a hundred dollars. No note or anything, just the envelope addressed to me and the money inside.

"Things like that happen all the time. It really blows my mind. I mean the Lord just always takes care of us."

"Sometimes he cuts it a little close," said a lanky, rather handsome young man who had just walked into the room. "He plays around with you a little."

"See what happens when you take dope?" Steve said to me, pointing at the newcomer. "You know when I was on the force I used to frisk this guy regularly. He was the worst freak in the area."

The guy was Ron Winckler; twenty-two years old and a sort of young ringleader in the Drug Prevention Center, the staff member who emceed speaking or singing engagements, and who made certain the right people were manning the Hotline phones at the right times. His personal testimony was a grisly one.

"I was a freak," Ron said with a kind of rigid intensity. "I didn't fit in at school and I didn't really care. Timothy Leary was my hero and LSD was my obsession. I always wanted to get so flipped out that I would find some kind of peace of mind.

"I got busted when I was in high school and got kicked out, and for the next couple of months I just sort of hitch-hiked around a lot, not really knowing where I was going. Just kind of trying to escape.

"One time I took about forty dollars worth of LSD all at the same time and I had a trip that was a nightmare. It was horrible and it kept getting worse and worse. I can't describe it as anything but hell. The emotional horror of what could only be hell. And I figured, if hell is real, then God must be real. I guess that was the first time I really thought about it.

"But I was still lost—still looking for answers. When I finally came down off that trip I wandered on up to San Francisco. Haight-Ashbury was supposed to be *the* place. All I saw were speed freaks who were so flipped out, they'd kill for five dollars. And I talked to the Hare Krishna kids and they said they had the answer for my life, but all they seemed to have was an eternal void.

"I was constantly having flashbacks from my bad LSD trips and they were worse than the trips themselves. Like one time I was eating a hamburger in a restaurant, and I looked at the hamburger and it was me! I was eating myself!"

As Ron spoke, he became more and more intense. If the point he was trying to make was that his life was an agony, he was making the point with unquestionable precision.

"But at the same time, there were all those little hints

being thrown at me. Like one time I was looking at a sign in the window of a drugstore that said 'Serve yourself and save.' I read it over and over and it seemed to say, 'Save yourself and serve.' I couldn't figure that out, but I couldn't get it out of my head. Or other times, I'd hear songs and they'd seem to have specific meanings for me. Like the Beatles—'Don't You Need Somebody to Love?' And I would be thinking, yes, I do need someone to love. But I can't figure out who, or what, or where.

"Then finally, I hitchhiked home and I got picked up by this guy who was a Christian. We were talking for a while—I was telling him all the things I had been into, and I admitted that nothing had really been the answer for me. He told me that Jesus Christ was the absolute truth and the only truth, and all that other stuff was heading in the wrong direction. And eventually, he said 'Ron, do you want to pray?' And I said I'd try. I said out loud. 'God, I believe in you and I believe Jesus Christ is the absolute truth and I'm putting all my faith in you.' "

"Then I stopped praying, and nothing happened. I didn't feel any different.

"But that night I went home—it was the first time I had been home in months—and in a split instant, I experienced God. I really had a physical feeling of God alive inside me, and all the loneliness and fears just poured out. I was in my room and I started praying again. I'd hear voices saying 'Don't pray, you fool. What are you wasting your time on your knees for. Stop it!' But I just fought the voices off and kept praying all night long. And I won the battle. I became a true Christian."

It seemed to me that LSD trips—bad ones—were often springboards into the new Christianity of the young. A non-Christian explained that when people explored their innermost consciousness with mind-expanding drugs, they were susceptible to feelings of great emotion and ecstasy, and they could easily attach those feelings to a religion—certainly to a religion which preached love, life after death, and a kind of eternal "high" in heaven.

But a Christian said to me, yes, LSD did bring a lot of kids to know Jesus in a kind of roundabout way. But so what? Who are we to question the way God chooses to work?

Two pretty interesting explanations. I could take my choice.

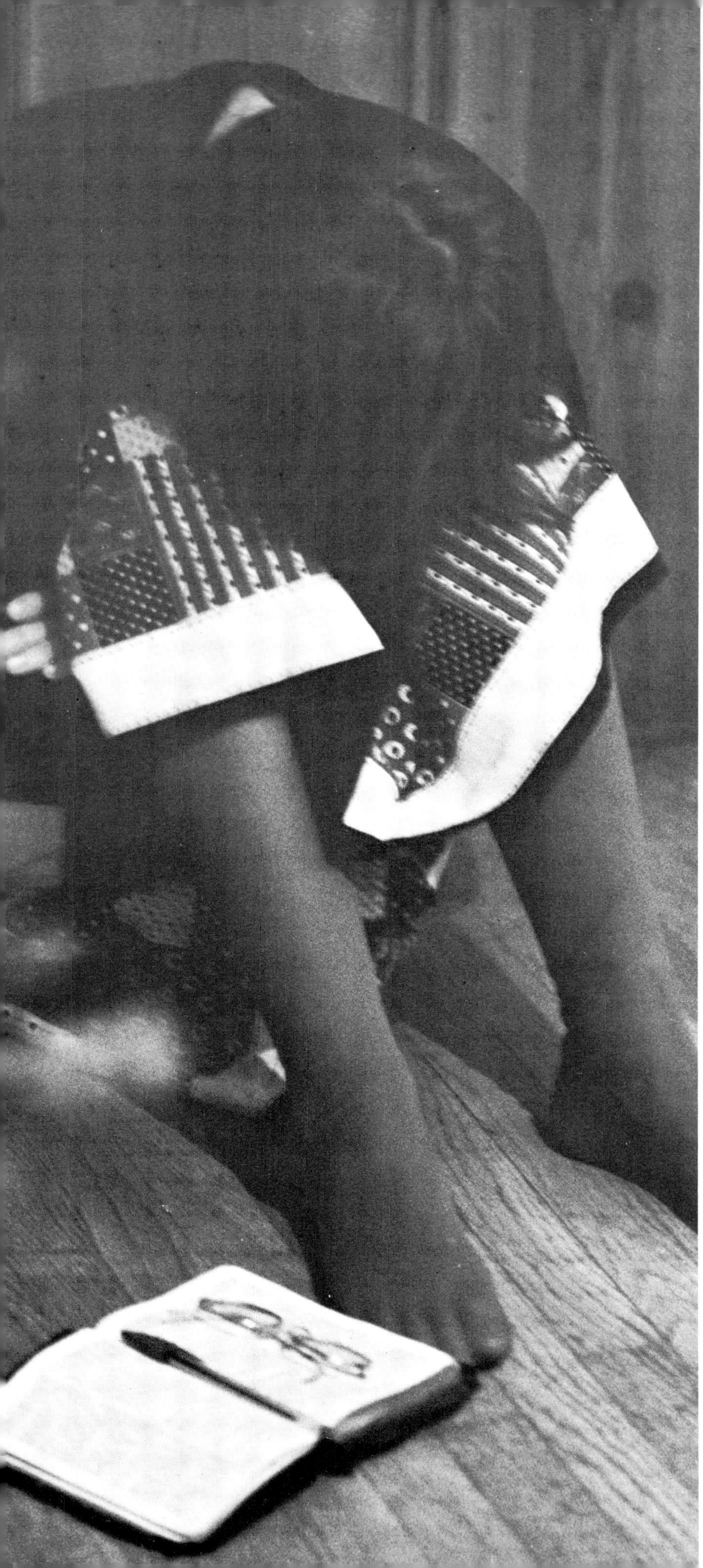

Rod Walker was the other male staff member of the Melodyland Drug Prevention Center. Only eighteen years old, he is one of the young people George Wakeling has unofficially added to his family. Rod had been a practicing, devout Christian for over two years and that qualified him for a role of spiritual elder among the young congregation that gravitates toward Melodyland. He also qualifies as house peacekeeper. Once, I was talking to him in his room at the Wakeling home and he was explaining the barbells that were on the floor. He said that he wasn't out for body-building or anything, but that he liked to use the weights to work off extra tension. While he was telling me this, he was absently toying with a forty-pound barbell the way I sometimes toy with my ballpoint pen. Rod is six-foot-six, about 220 pounds, and to use a butcher's term, there's not much wastage.

But he, too, found Christ after first finding himself in an unpleasant LSD experience.

"When I was sixteen, I was into a little bit of everything. First football, and then that got boring. Then I started drinking with the guys, and that got old, and then I got into drugs.

"One night, I had a really bad LSD trip, and when I came down, I was really spaced out. For the next two days, I was completely messed up and helpless. I was having flashbacks and I was kind of terrified all the time.

"One night I woke up, and I was flashing again, and I needed something to turn my mind off. I went over to my parents' tape recorder and turned it on. I don't know what made me do it, I just did. There was a tape on talking about being a Christian and stuff. I don't even remember exactly what it said, but that night I accepted Jesus and that's what got it started. That was two and a half years ago."

Here was the chance to ask the question that was constantly on my mind. The thing that had been bothering me ever since I started taking a longer look at the Jesus Movement. Does it have any staying power? Of course when someone is flashing on a bad trip and someone else holds out a promise of peace, he's going to grab it. But how does it hold up in time, especially with a kid like Rod who could probably be a top athlete in any sport and was obviously a young man with his head very much together. Jesus was there when he needed him, maybe. But what about now when he doesn't seem to need any particular support?

"I feel more solid with Christ now than I ever did before," Rod said evenly. "I just keep growing as a Christian as I learn more about him.

"People say I belong in the ministry, but I don't know. It's hard to decide. I know God has a plan for my life, but I guess I have to figure it out through trial and error. I know I'm not going to hear voices or anything. I just have to go out and try to do what's right for me. God knows I love Him, so there's no problem there."

I liked talking to Rod. There was nothing Jesus-freaky about him. He was easy and natural. I asked him if there was ever a possibility of his going back to his old life—not taking drugs necessarily, but living with God somewhere other than in the middle of his life.

"You really can't go back," Rod said. "I know. I tried. But once you come to know God, you just can't go against Him. You just know it's too stupid."

"So God is the center of your life," I said. "How do you spend your spare time?"

"Well yesterday, Ron and I went down to the Navy brig to testify to prisoners."

"How did it go?"

"Oh, it went well."

"What does 'well' mean?"

"It means they didn't throw anything at us," Rod said grinning.

"Okay, that brings up another question I've been wondering about. You and the other members of the Drug Prevention Center's Speakers' Bureau, you go around and testify, right?"

"That's right."

"In other words, you tell about what your life used to be and then about how you accepted Jesus and how he has changed you, right?"

"Yes."

"And how many times do you do that?"

"Sometimes once a week. Sometimes five times in a single day. It depends on the schedule."

"And you've been doing that for about two years now, right?"

"Yes."

"Doesn't it ever get *boring*?"

I thought I was asking a trick question, but it was pretty quickly obvious that I wasn't.

"I'd be a liar if I said it didn't sometimes get boring. Telling people how screwed up you were and then how you were saved. And knowing that most of the time you're talking to people who aren't paying any attention to you anyway.

"But I guess it's like parents raising their children. They're not always overjoyed to be taking care of them all the time. But they love them, so they do it. I love God. So I testify. And when I get a little bored, I pray for some extra strength."

The female member of the Drug Prevention Center at Anaheim was Donna Sturgill, and to me she was someone special. The first time I met her, I asked if she would give me her testimony, just the way she would if she was speaking at a school assembly or something. (The Supreme Court, incidentally, never ruled against giving testimony in schools. Just praying.)

Donna said sure, and we went into an empty office and closed the door and she started talking. When she was seventeen, she was average-looking, she said, and was getting average grades in school, and was a bored churchgoer and social wallflower.

To break the monotonous pattern that was beginning to grow around her, she started going to bars with her friends, and pretty soon that was a nightly habit, and life was a big party. And then there was the party where the first joint was passed around. And Donna was leery, but she tried it anyway. And she liked it.

So the drinker graduated into grass, and she began taking whites to wake herself up and reds to bring herself down and she was sniffing speed in between.

"But I wasn't worried. I saw friends around me who were getting really freaked out by drugs, but I knew I could handle mine. I knew I could take care of myself.

"But after a while it was getting to be like I was in a giant circle. I was just running around, burning myself up. And I was wondering, where does it all *stop?*

"One night I was lying in bed and I couldn't go to sleep. I had taken a couple of reds and smoked some marijuana, and I wasn't even stoned. I was just lying there, and I started taking an inventory of myself. 'Okay, Donna. You're nineteen years old. You have no job. No real friends. No real home life. No future. Where do you go from here? And what do you do when you get there?'

"And I didn't have an answer!"

As Donna was telling me this, it was as if she were telling someone her story for the first time. She was talking with so much emotion, she was almost on the edge of tears, as if she was reliving that horrible moment in her life. But at the same time, she looked so untouched by anything tainted or lurid. The words and the experiences seemed so incongruous with the person.

"That night is when it happened," she continued. "I got out of bed and got on my knees and said 'God, if You're really there and do everything everyone says You do, then take away this desire I have for drugs. You know now that I can't face the outside world without drugs. I'm afraid of it. So if You are really real, please, *please* take this away. Because dear God if You don't understand me and can't help me, who can?'

"I stayed on my knees praying for two hours, and suddenly I felt clean inside, clean for the first time since I could remember. I knew then and there that I had changed and that my life would never be the same again.

"The next day I saw some of my friends and they asked me what had happened. They said I looked different.

"I said, you're going to think I'm nuts, but last night I decided to believe in Christ as my Lord and Savior.

"They said they thought I was nuts.

"I kept going to parties after that. I went to witness to the people there—to try to show them how God had changed my life and how He could change theirs. One time a guy took me into a bedroom and pointed to a spread filled with reds and grass and every kind of drug. And he said 'Help yourself.' But I said 'No thank you. I don't need them anymore.' And I didn't.

"But I kept witnessing. A few of my friends came to Jesus, and that was such a blessing. Because I wanted everyone to know what the Lord can do. And how about you?"

The question was out of nowhere.

" 'How about me' what?" I said, knowing darn well what.

Instead of asking again, Donna reached into a desk and pulled out a small paperback copy of the New Testament. "Will you take this and read it if you get a chance?"

I felt like I was being let off the hook, but I promised her I would. Then we talked about other things—how the Hotline worked, and how many calls came in each day, and what the typical problems were—that kind of stuff.

Eventually, I had to leave, and I said good-by to Donna and started the drive to my motel. About five miles out, I remembered that I had forgotten the New Testament I had promised to read, and I returned to her office to get it. Mostly, because I liked her and didn't want to hurt her feelings.

She was standing at the door with the small book in her hand when I returned. I was going to say something like "I forgot my . . ." but she just handed it to me and smiled that incredible secret smile that so many Christians seem to have, and said simply, "Praise the Lord."

It was almost a year later that I saw Donna and Ron and Rod, George Wakeling, and Steve Kosca again. I returned to Melodyland and walked into the beginning of a Tuesday evening youth service. The huge round amphitheater was partitioned off so that a fraction of its space was used for the evening. Several parents and several hundred kids —straight and hippie and in-between—sat waiting for the service to begin.

It started as a sort of updated, supercharged version of the adult evening service I had seen a year earlier—the one conducted by Pastor Wilkerson with the seemingly inspirationless hymn-singing and the keeling-over bit at the end.

This service began with hymns also, but they were uptempo, accompanied by a piano that bordered on rag-

67

time. The regular Tuesday night congregation sang lustily, while newcomers mouthed the words when they knew them and looked around a little nervously—not at all certain what was going to happen. Some of the newcomers probably had promised to attend the meeting after making an emergency call to the Hotline. Others, perhaps, were coming because their friends did.

But most of the congregation were steady customers, and when George Wakeling walked up to the round stage and invited people to share the good things that had happened to them during the week, the response was immediate and slightly breathless.

"My sister had a bad trial with our parents last week," one sixteen-year-old girl began. "She came out of the house crying and she came up to me and said, 'Sue, I've lost my bike, and the folks will kill me if they find out.' And so I said we should pray and we did. 'Lord, you've just got to help us find that bike, please. And if it's not there when we go look, just create one, okay? 'Cause we've really got to have it.'"

As the girl was talking, she was bouncing up and down on her heels, literally bubbling. "We walked down the street for a way and then turned the corner and bang! There it was. We really rejoiced to the Lord about that."

"Praise God," everyone said.

Then another girl stood up. She was about the same age, dressed in jeans and a polka-dot blouse, and if anything, she was even more exuberant than her predecessor.

"I had this cyst-like thing on my eye, you know?" She said to the politely attentive congregation. "And it was really a burden, you know? Because I couldn't see straight and I was getting dizzy a lot and stuff.

"So I prayed to the Lord about it, you know? I just said, Jesus, please make my eye feel better so I can feel more like praising your name. And you know? The next morning the cyst thing was gone!

"I used to think that, well, if God felt like doing something for ya, He would. But if He didn't, you know, like if He had more important stuff, He'd just ignore you. But now I know, you know, that God will do *anything!*"

I couldn't help thinking about the Pentacostals in Bethel Tabernacle—the prayers in tongues who were almost grim in comparison with this breezy, middle-class group of kids. I wouldn't dare hazard a guess about which group had more religion, but it was sure obvious which group had more problems. When someone at Bethel gave

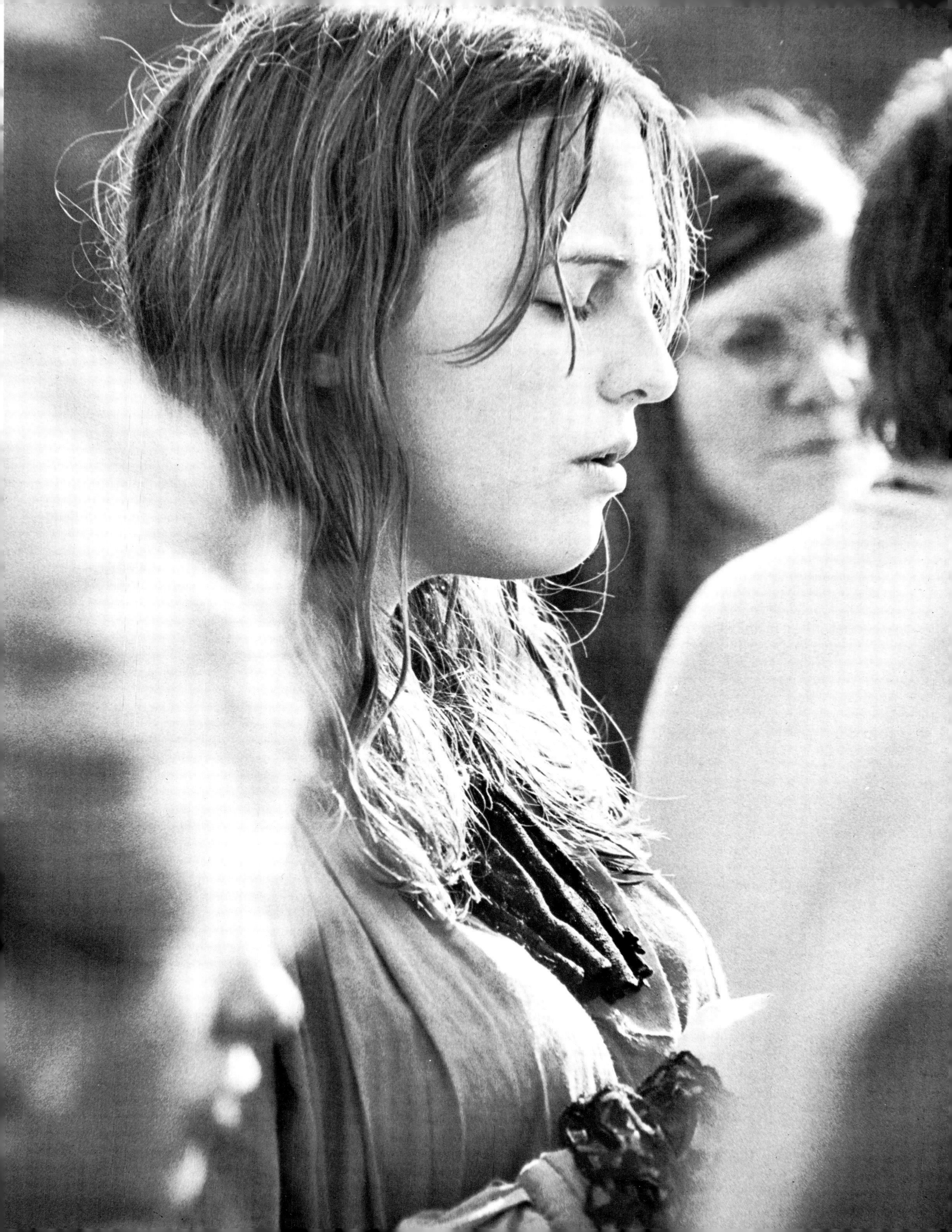

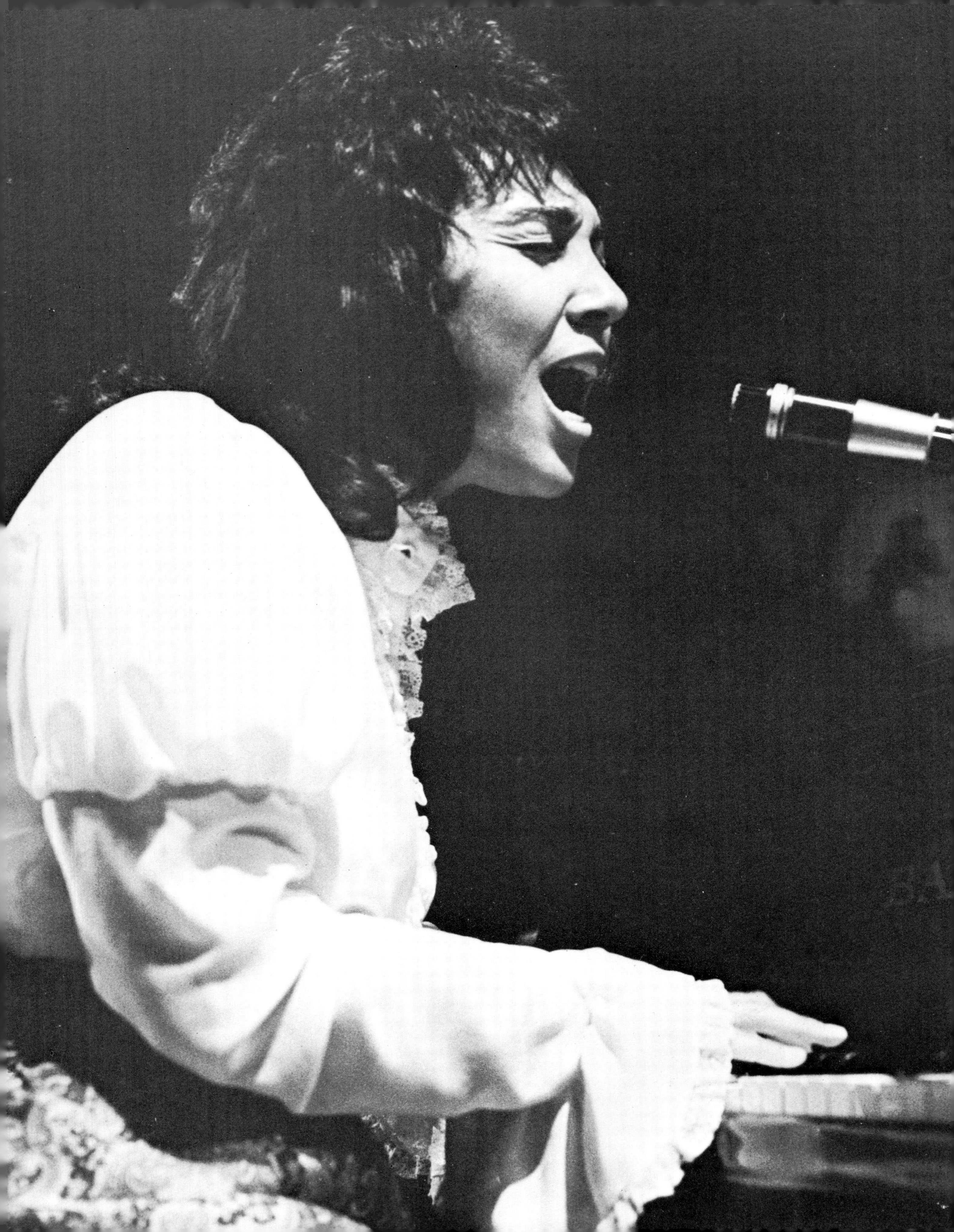

witness, he might easily be telling about getting hepatitis from the dirty hypodermic needle he used to puncture his last good arm vein, loading up on heroin. And then, he might say he prayed to Jesus as he lay dying and was miraculously cured. That would be fairly standard testimony at Bethel.

So my first reaction was that these girls were being silly—a lost bicycle, an eye cyst. I mean, wouldn't God seriously have better things to do? And that was the first time, the very first time in a very long time, that I thought about God *doing* anything. And I decided that if I was going to admit He could cure heroin addiction, I would have to admit He could do anything, big or small. Cure an eye cyst? Why not? It was a strange train of thought that probably would have kept going had I not heard my name mentioned.

George Wakeling was announcing on the stage that Jack and Betty Cheetham and I were attending the service. And he said that Jack and Betty had both been saved and filled with the Holy Spirit while they were recording the Jesus Movement with their cameras.

"And I ask you people out there now to praise God for these three people, because they were obedient."

And I thought, *obedient?*

"They were doing God's work and they helped bring many, many people to the Lord. We praise You, God, for doing Your work through them."

I didn't want to think about that idea at all, and I began scribbling in my notebook urgently. "The amphitheater is round," I wrote. "The lady next to me coughed. The major attraction this evening will be Carrie's Company—a new singing group. The lady next to me coughed again."

Carrie's Company is Carrie Gonzalo, 27-year-old Filipino beauty, her husband, three cousins, and four friends.

Their music was semi-rock, semi-soul with Carrie at the piano crooning or shouting into a lowered microphone the lyrics of the new music—Jesus music.

>*I'll never be the same again, no no.*
>*I'll never be the same again, no no.*
>*Since my soul was saved,*
>*I'll glory in serving the Lord,*
>*And I'll never be the same again, oh no.*

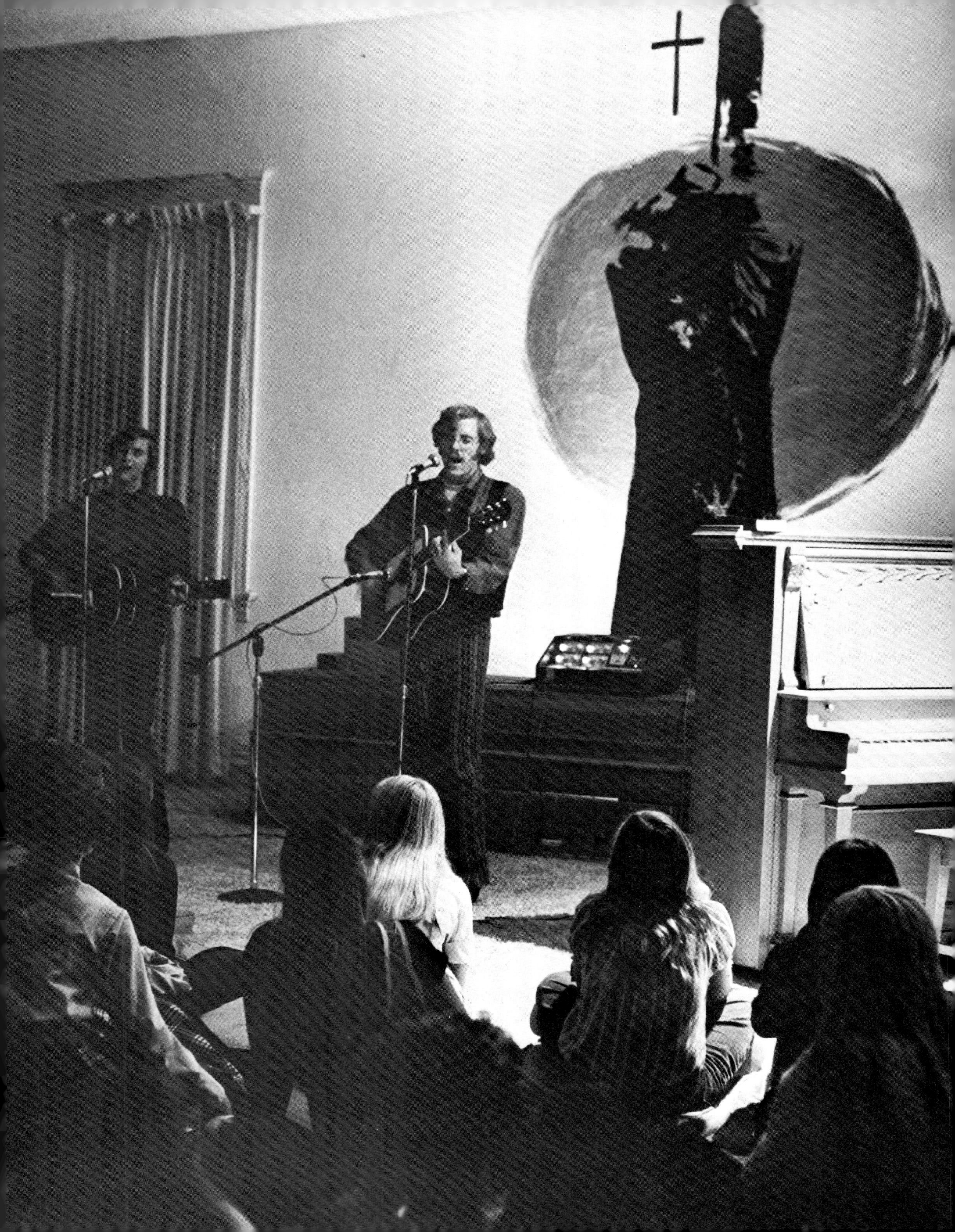

After each number, some of the congregation clapped, but most pointed their forefingers into the air—giving the new Christian high sign. The first Christians, I was always taught, made their identities known by making the sign of a fish with their toe in the sand. The new Christians are not nearly so furtive. They say hello, goodby, and give appreciation by pointing skyward, signifying "One Way—His Way" with their half a peace symbol.

Between some of the songs, members of Carrie's Company would step forward to give a little short personal testimony.

"It means a lot to have Jesus in your heart," said a black-eyed, flowing-haired girl who would have to stand tiptoe to reach five feet. "It means a lot to me. Epecially since I work in the complaint department at Sears." (Laughter.) "Jesus is really my companion all the time. He said 'My peace I give to you, my peace I leave unto you.' I really need that peace to keep me from losing my temper, and Jesus gives it to me. I really love him for that."

Donna came up the aisle and sat next to me during the singing. She looked just about the way she looked a year earlier—maybe lovelier, and I told her so. "That's silly," she said. "If you see anything lovely in me, it's the Lord."

We listened to the music for a while and then the featured speaker of the evening came out on the stage. "You'll love him," Donna said. "He's really a terrific speaker. He really has the power of the Spirit working in him."

The speaker was Robert Larson, a lean, blond, twenty-three-year-old who had recently opened a storefront ministry in a tough section of Pacific Beach, a suburb of San Diego. His message for the evening was sin—not necessarily the evil of sin or the punishment for sin—but almost the inevitability of sin and the payment for it that has already been made.

"On the cross of Christ, God paid for our sins," Larson said, his high tenor filling the vast room. "The blood of Christ satisfies God. If you confess before God—every sin past and future is forgiven."

Larson was no Bible thumper. He kept his listeners listening by being personal, and talking their language. "I sin, man. Maybe I'll grab a smoke, or swear at something or tell a lie, and the Devil will come up to me and say, 'Larson, how can you do all that preaching about Jesus Christ when you're just an old sinner yourself. Man, that's *hypocritical.*' But I'm justified freely in the faith of his blood. Do you understand what I'm saying?

"Sometimes I pray to the Lord and I say, 'Lord, I'm really going to repent this time. I'm not going to mess around anymore. You're looking at the *new* Larson.' Then I sail out the door and smack! Right on my face. I'm a sinner. I can't handle myself. But it's okay, man. Because God has already forgiven me. I'm free.

"And it feels so good to be free. Doesn't it?"

"Amen," a few offer timidly.

"*Doesn't it?*" Larson challenges.

"Aaaa*men.*" they respond.

"Right," says Larson. "And if there is anyone in this room who has anything to live for outside Christ, let me see him raise his hand." A few very young children, reacting with the Pavlovian instincts of grammar school, raised their hands. Their mothers quickly yanked the hands down.

"Praise *God*," Larson said, pleased with the otherwise nonresponding audience. "Because what *is* there to live for besides Jesus Christ?"

Then Larson read a letter which he said had been written by a young Communist in Mexico who was breaking his engagement with his sweetheart because "all I want to live for is Communism."

"And if he feels that way toward *Communism*, shouldn't we feel ten thousand times more zealous about Christ?" Larson shouted. "I challenge you to dedicate your life to Christ. I *challenge* you to make that commitment. And tonight is the *night!*

"Let's bow our heads in prayer right now," Larson said now soothingly. All heads went down. "Now with all heads bowed, how many of you can say tonight you know the feeling of total freedom in Christ? Raise your hands."

I took a peek around the auditorium. About two-thirds of the three hundred or so in the congregation signified they enjoyed that freedom.

"Is there anyone here tonight who does not know Christ but would like to?" Larson asked. Donna took a quick look over at me but I was writing furiously.

"Is there *anyone* out there who would like to come to know Christ tonight?" Larson asked again. No response.

"Are there any of you out there who feel condemned all the time?" A few raised hands.

"Jesus, set these people free tonight," Larson implored

with his face lifted, and then looking out at the audience he said, "I see your hands. Yes. I see your hands.

"Now anyone who wants to dedicate his life more fully to Jesus Christ, those of you with your hands raised, come up here now. Come on. Get out of your seats and come up here right now. All of you. That's right. Come up now." This was the altar call. Practically every service in the wave of new Christians has one. It is a call for new converts to be saved, or in this case, for former converts to make a public reaffirmation of their faith—a "booster shot" someone jokingly called it later. But the most important thing about it is that it is public. You have to stand up there with people watching you and say, "yes, I'm a sinner. I admit it publicly before God."

The first time I saw an altar call, I figured the young minister was saying to himself, "If Billy Graham and Rex Humbard can do it, by God I can do it." The words always seemed to share a monotonous sameness. "Tonight is the night. Now is the time for you to make your decision. Right now. Get out of your seat and come." And I also was suspicious of the approach. Persons were always asked to raise their hands while all heads were bowed as their first admission that they wanted the promised new life. Then, with their hands raised, they were asked to come forward. It seemed to me kind of like a trick.

But every time I brought up this objection, it was explained to me plainly and patiently that the *only* important thing was getting people to accept Christ as their Savior and repent for their sins. The how of getting people in that situation is unimportant. It's *getting* people that counts. And evidently the new Christians use the altar call because, they say, in the past it's done the job. It has worked.

But Bob Larson's altar call this night was something very different and for me, a little unsettling. The young people who had gone up to the altar had already 'been saved' but now they were preparing themselves for a second experience—the Baptism of the Holy Spirit.

I vaguely remembered someone telling me a person could have two Baptisms—the Baptism of water and that of the Holy Spirit. The second, I was told, gave Christians greater power and strength in their faith, and it could often occur when hands of a strong believer were laid on the head of the one to receive the Baptism.

What precisely it was, I didn't know. The Christians

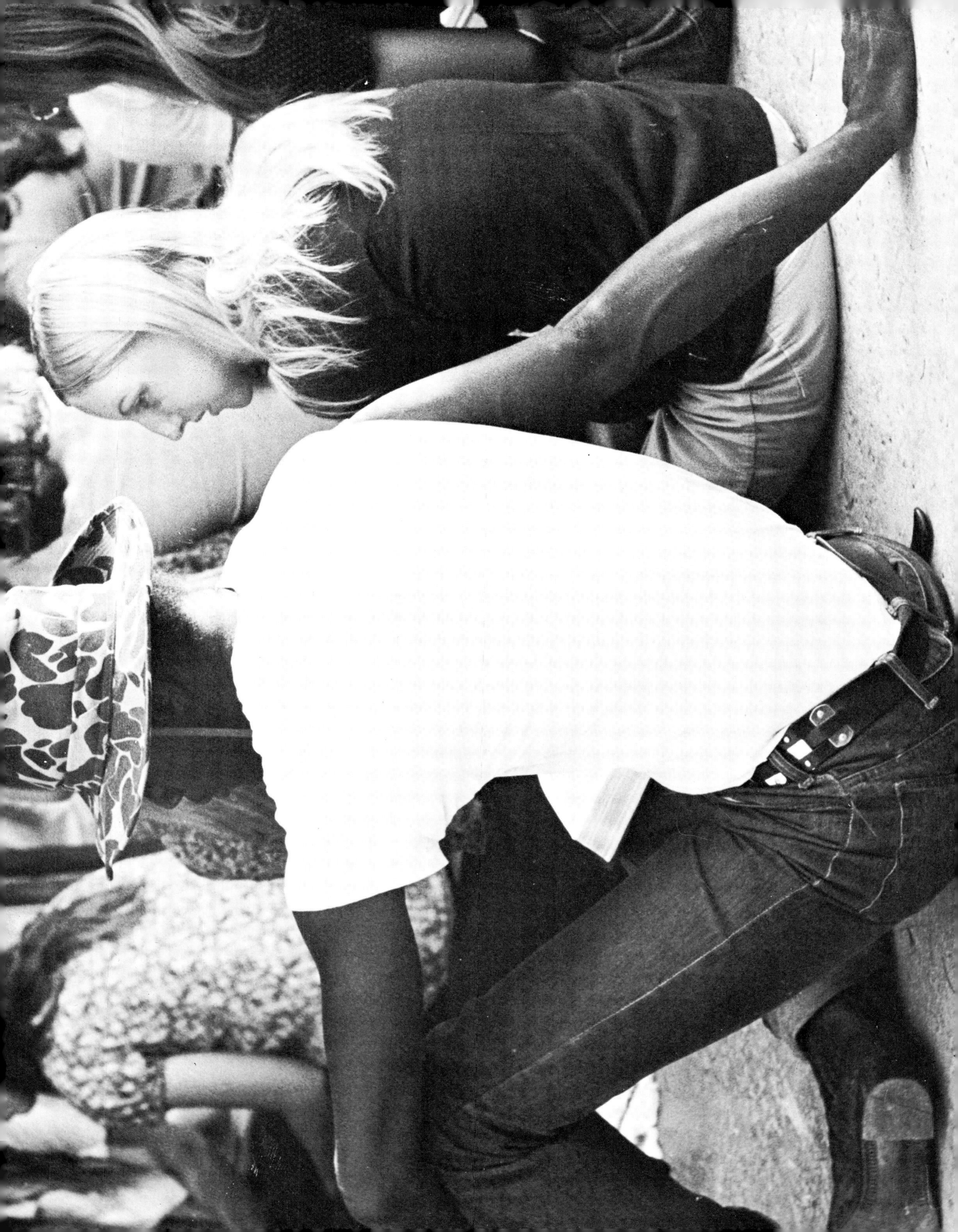

said it was the power of the Holy Spirit entering a person's body. That wasn't really very descriptive for me. The Holy Spirit had always been the vague member of the triumvirate. I was always able to picture him only as a slightly obscure flicker of flame or a plump white dove. Watching Bob Larson, I got a better idea of this supposed union.

About a dozen young people had answered this altar call and as they approached the rounded stage, counselors —others who had been Christians for some time and who had been taught to assist at services—came up behind them.

Larson stood before each person and prayed over him, a little in English, a little in tongues, "Oh Jesus, halleluia, praise you Jesus, praise you Lord, ala ca mea, kea malici mea ola kala, oh praise you Jesus, give her the Holy Spirit, Father."

The intensity was electric. Larson's loud forceful, beseeching was accompanied by the counselors who were praying out loud themselves, also half in English and half in tongues.

As Larson's prayers reached a certain peak of constructed tension, he would put his hands on the person

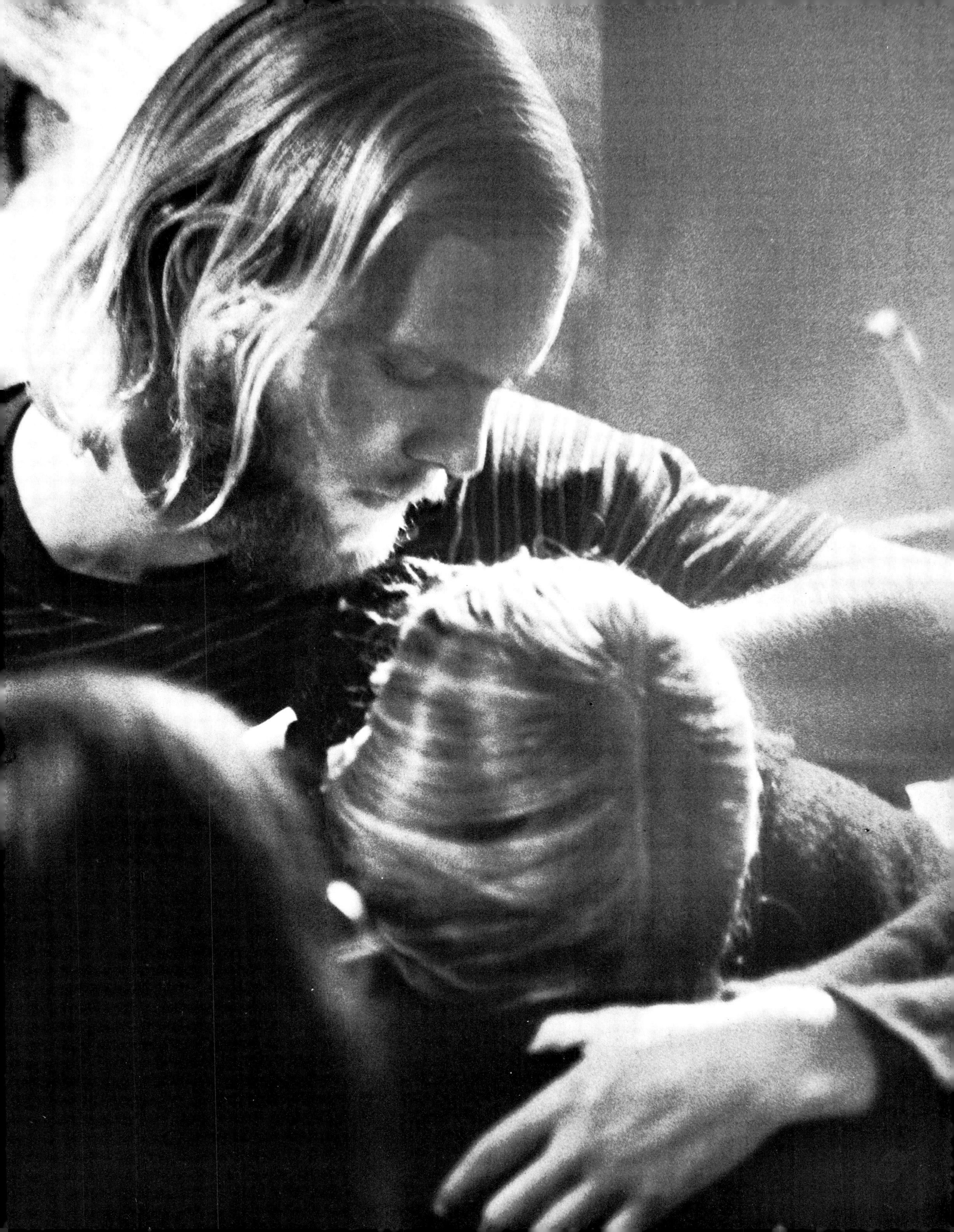

he was praying for. Some would fall over backward to be caught in the waiting arms of the counselors. Others would begin to gyrate and cry out loudly, "Thank you Jesus. Oh thank you, thank you Jesus."

One young girl, dressed in a long flowered dress, was prayed over for several minutes. Larson prayed for her loudly with his head raised, and several counselors surrounded her with their arms on her shoulders praying fervently. "Oh Holy Spirit, come to her now. Come to her. Oh praise Jesus. Praise Jesus."

The girl was kneeling, slightly bent over, and then suddenly she threw her head back and shouted "Oh God! Oh my precious God! Oh thank you Jesus," and tears were streaming down her cheeks and her face was absolute ecstasy. The counselors kept their hands on her. After a few moments she sprang to her feet and hugged them: "My God! I never thought it would be like that! I never dreamed anything could be that fantastic. Oh praise Jesus!"

The counselors were smiling and hugging her and one said, "didn't we tell you?" And the girl kept saying over and over, "yes, oh yes, but I never dreamed! Oh thank you Jesus. Thank you Jesus."

Not all those who had come to the altar were there for the Baptism. One sixteen-year-old girl wearing jeans, a puff-sleeved white blouse and no shoes had come up, she said, because she couldn't free herself from a feeling of guilt. Larson prayed over her for a few moments and then touched her forehead and moved on. She remained kneeling at the altar a while, a little tomboyish blonde looking very much alone. And then she began to cry—slowly at first, and then openly, unreservedly like an infant.

Donna and another counselor immediately came to her and knelt on either side and put their arms around her.

"Oh He'll never come. He'll never come," the girl sobbed.

"God loves you," Donna said.

"Oh no, He doesn't. He can't. I just sin all the time. Oh God!"

I was watching, feeling real fear in my stomach. The girl seemed on the verge of a genuine emotional breakdown. Her sobs seemed to come from a tortured soul.

"He'll never come! He'll never come!"

But Donna was being very firm and looking directly at the girl. "He will!" she said. "God loves you."

"No," the girl cried. "There's something inside me that won't let Him come. Something bad inside me."

Donna and the other counselor exchanged a glance, a worried, knowing look as if there were unexpected trouble that had to be dealt with immediately.

Then they went into action, like two spiritual surgeons going into an emergency operation. They began praying alternately, firmly, aggressively.

"Right now. I pray in Jesus' name," Donna said. "That something get out of you and be gone."

"No, no," the girl sobbed. "I can't. I can't."

"Nothing can stand up against the power of the Lord," the other counselor said.

"Oh no. I can't. Oh please."

"Jesus, come now!" Donna said. The girl began bending over, as if she was in great pain. "In Jesus' name, I ask You God. Come now. Come now. I ask in Jesus' name."

"Oh please," the girl sobbed. "Oh Jesus, please help me. I need your help. Please help."

The two counselors exchanged another glance, and then looked cautiously at the girl between them. She was crying freely now, easily, and her words were flowing out with traces of relief. "Help me Jesus. You know I need you. You know I love you."

Then it happened—a moment that came and went before I realized it. But I could see that something very specific had happened to the girl. A crisis had really arrived and passed. Donna told me later she had been "delivered." All I could see was that some positive change had happened to her. Her tears gradually became a shower of gratitude and then relief and joy. This little girl who before had seemed to have an old, pained face was now a little girl again.

"Thank you Jesus," she whispered, and Donna and the other counselor looked up to the ceiling and repeated the simple words of gratitude. Then the hugging began again, but this was not the hugging of sheer ecstasy I had seen earlier. This was hugging of reassurance. "You see?" Donna said to the girl. "There's just no power greater than the power of Jesus. There just isn't."

The service was over. Without my noticing, almost everyone in the room had left. George Wakeling's daughter Leslie came over to where I was sitting, grinning almost absurdly.

"What happened to you?" I said.

"I made the altar call," she answered. "I just needed a little spiritual recharging. And oh, it feels so good!"

Leslie had always struck me as being very much like her father. She seemed to exude down-to-earth common sense. But here she was, giggling, an engaging but thoroughly adolescent teeny-bopper.

"I always forget," she said. "I just forget how *good* it feels."

Donna and the girl came over from the altar, and they both hugged Leslie and smiled that smile. I was feeling very left out. There was something good going on, and I definitely wasn't in on it.

"How do you feel," I said to the girl, pretty much just for something to say.

"I feel like a chain that's been binding me was just broken," she said. "I don't feel like scum anymore. I don't feel like a black sheep in God's family."

"You never were," Donna said to her. "That's the thing you have to say to yourself over and over. You never were."

Everywhere I went in southern California, trying to get my hands on this revival, I was told that I had to go to Calvary Chapel. That was where amazing things were really happening, I was told. That was where more people were being won for Christ than anywhere.

I called my local directory assistant to get an address for this miracle house.

"Information, for what city please?"

"I don't know, operator," I said. "That's kind of why I'm calling. I'm looking for a Calvary Chapel, somewhere outside Los Angeles."

"I have several listings for churches and chapels called 'Calvary,'" the operator said.

"Well I'm afraid . . ."

"But you must mean the one in Costa Mesa."

"Oh?"

"That's where the Lord is really moving in a powerful way."

"Oh."

"Thank you for calling, sir. And God bless you."

That really happened.

And obviously Calvary was a bastion of this movement that had to be explored. I visited the chapel in Costa Mesa and was introduced to Chuck Smith, the senior minister there, a big, balding man who looked like a cross between a head football coach and an airline pilot. He also looked like an almost exaggerated father figure. I started to interview him and I almost wanted to climb up on his lap. Instead I asked him the only thing I could think of. What did he think of the Jesus Movement?

"What do I think of it? I think it's like a tidal wave coming in. It's Jesus. And he's moving.

"Wherever we go, or send people, to open up Christian houses, they're getting filled up immediately. And kids are coming not by the score, but by the hundreds. By the thousands.

"What do I attribute this tidal wave to? It's that these kids have gone the whole route. Where else is there for them to go? It's as if God has always been a last resort and now these kids have gone full cycle back to Him.

"In school, they've been taught the relativity of everything. No absolutes. Absolutely no absolutes! Beginning with Kierkegaard in philosophy and then into the arts, music, and finally theology. The theory that God is dead.

"These kids are exposed on all levels to the nothingness of everything. And then we come along and assert, yes! There are absolutes. Yes, there is a pattern, and yes, there is a design. Yes, we are approaching the end of the earth, and here is something you can hold on to, something that is true and lasting and has foreseen it all.

"And you can read it all here," Smith said, slapping his Bible. "Here is exactly where you are, and here is the next step, and yes, there is hope.

"Kids have been robbed all along the way. We come along and give them a hope and a purpose."

The Wednesday night youth meetings at Calvary Chapel give animated proof that what Smith is offering is being quickly, totally accepted. The chapel is relatively small, with a listed capacity of 522 persons... stained wood pews, green shag carpets below, peaked beam ceiling above. The altar in front is a stage with steps leading up to it from the middle aisle.

At about five p.m. on Wednesdays, cars begin to fill the parking lot—cars with bumper-stickers that say things like "Things Go Better with Christ" and "Find Help Fast in the Bible Pages" and "Have a Nice Eternity." By seven-thirty, when the service is scheduled to begin, the lot is filled to capacity, and cars are parked bumper-sticker to bumper-sticker for blocks down every street within a mile of the Chapel. The 522-person ruling is routinely overlooked. Kids sit in the aisles, cram into the back vestibule, and spill out by the hundreds onto a side patio. They are good-looking kids, lots of bearded faces, some black ones, and shoes always the exception rather than the rule.

The first service I attended was conducted by Chuck Smith, Jr., the pastor's twenty-year-old son who was sporting shoulder-length hair, flared jeans, a velour shirt and sneakers.

"I'm here tonight because the regular youth minister—Lonnie Frisbee, had to be at a service in the Hollywood Bowl," Chuck began. "I know he leads you in singing and it's great because he can really get it going.

"For me, it's a bummer. I can't sing. Around the house, they won't even let me open my mouth. When I start quietly singing, praising the Lord around home, someone always tells me to shut up. That's how bad my voice is. When I sing a hymn, it's almost a sacrilege."

It was almost like an opening comedy monologue the young minister was giving, but it worked. Chuck had set the tone for the evening—light—and he had thoroughly won over his audience. Now, he moved easily into his message.

"Too many of us are on a pride trip.'Look at me. I'm a Christian. Wow!'

"But how about the words to the hymn, 'How Great Thou Art.' That's where it's at. How great the Lord is. Not us."

Then came time for testimony. Chuck asked if anyone had anything to share with the rest. An 18-year-old girl stood up and said: "I'd like to share with you that it was two weeks ago that I got born again."

The chapel became positively alive with good feeling. The joy was getting tangible again.

"I have a song to sing, and it's really my witness," she said. She came up to the stage, arranged herself and her worn guitar, and began to sing a lovely, lilting ballad that sounded something like this:

> *Funny how we all have changed,*
> *Trying desperately to know who we are.*
> *Well you don't have to look very far.*
> *Jesus—he's all around you.*
> *My head had been spinning 'round and 'round*
> *With Hare Hare Krishna Krishna*
> *But then one day I heard voices from a chapel*
> *And I was filled with fear.*
> *Jesus, I said, Jesus*
> *I know I have sinned. Please forgive me.*
> *And he did, I know he did.*
> *I sing my Savior's name.*
> *Alleluia. Alleluia.*

When she finished her song, the 1,500-kid congregation broke into spirited applause.

"And anyone out there who doesn't know Jesus," she called out over the clapping. "Man, I'm telling you you're missing *everything*. I'm high right now. I've never been so high in my life. On Jesus Christ!"

"Praise the Lord!" the congregation shouted almost in unison.

After the girl left the stage, other singing groups came on and the music lasted two hours. Then came the Bible study, conducted by Chuck Smith, Jr., and no one looked remotely restless. Most of the packed audience eagerly pulled out their own Bibles—a dazzling miscellany that ranged from fur-covered to paper tattered.

The Scripture for the evening was Genesis, chapter eighteen, and it was not read or discussed. It was rapped.

". . . Abraham said, 'Lord, don't get uptight with me, but what if I can only find fifty righteous people. Would you still destroy the city? . . . I mean, come on Lord . . . Suppose I can only find ten righteous people. Would that be it for the city Lord?' And the Lord said, 'You find ten righteous people, and I won't destroy the city. I'm going to split now, but I'll send you two angels to help out.' "

Chuck's teaching was frequently interrupted with laughter. The crowd obviously enjoyed studying their Bible his way, and he made the lessons amusing.

"You know there's sexual intercourse mentioned in the Bible. I'm not afraid to talk about it. After all, God invented it. And when they talk about sexual intercourse in the Bible, they say 'know' like this guy 'knew' his wife. And that's because when a man and his wife have sexual intercourse, they get to know each other better . . . Or at least that's what I've been told.

"But man, Satan can mess it all up and make sexual intercourse an evil thing. You know that.

"And you know how Satan comes around and tries to mess with you. He'll say, 'Man, you're too young. You have too much living to do to go around thinking about the Lord. Wait until you're about eighty and then maybe you might dig sitting around reading the Bible.

"Satan's trying to get our eyes off the Lord. And it's weird, the gimmicks he uses. He'll say, 'Hey, that was just a little sin, no sweat. That one's not worth Picadilly.'

"Satan talks that way sometimes.

"But man, there are no *little* sins. I know, you say you've heard that junk before. That little sins turn into

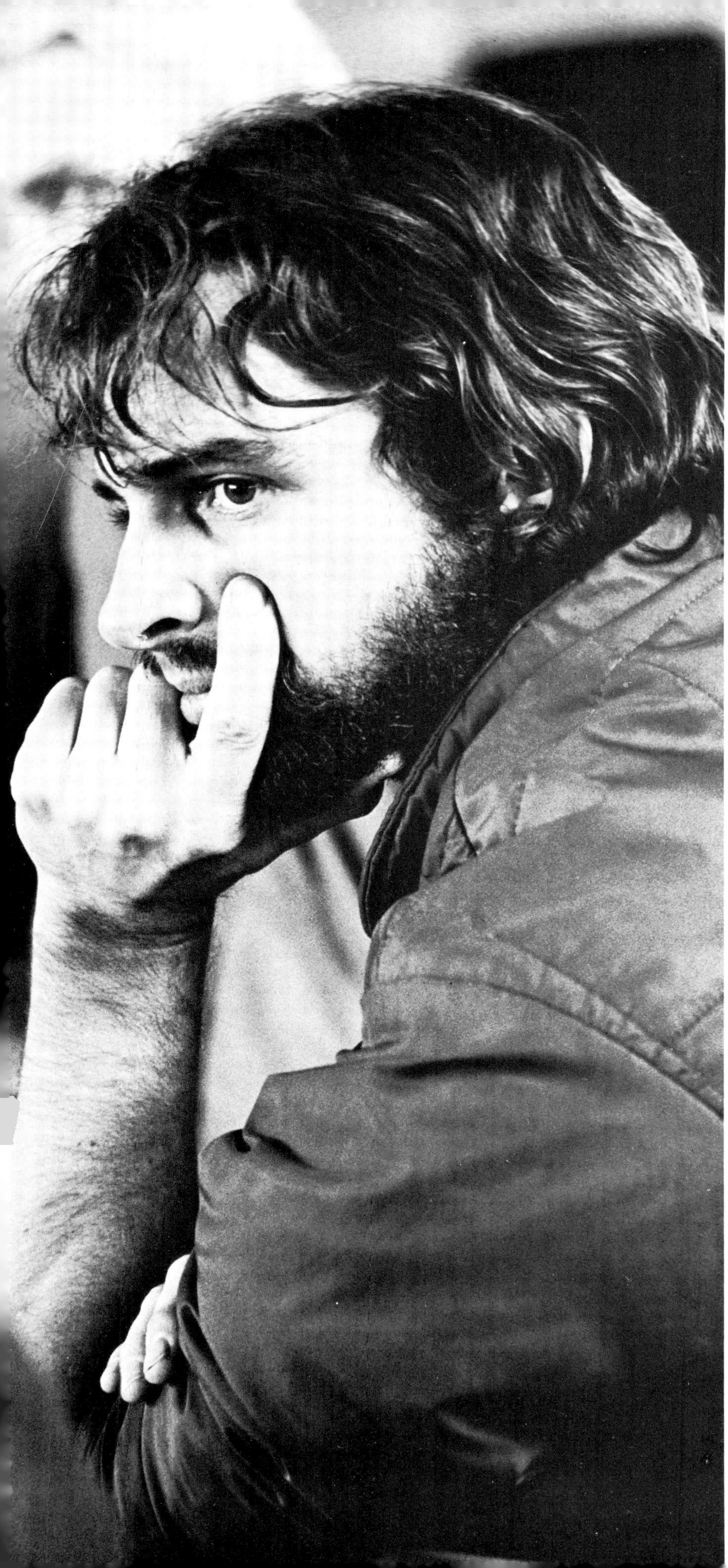

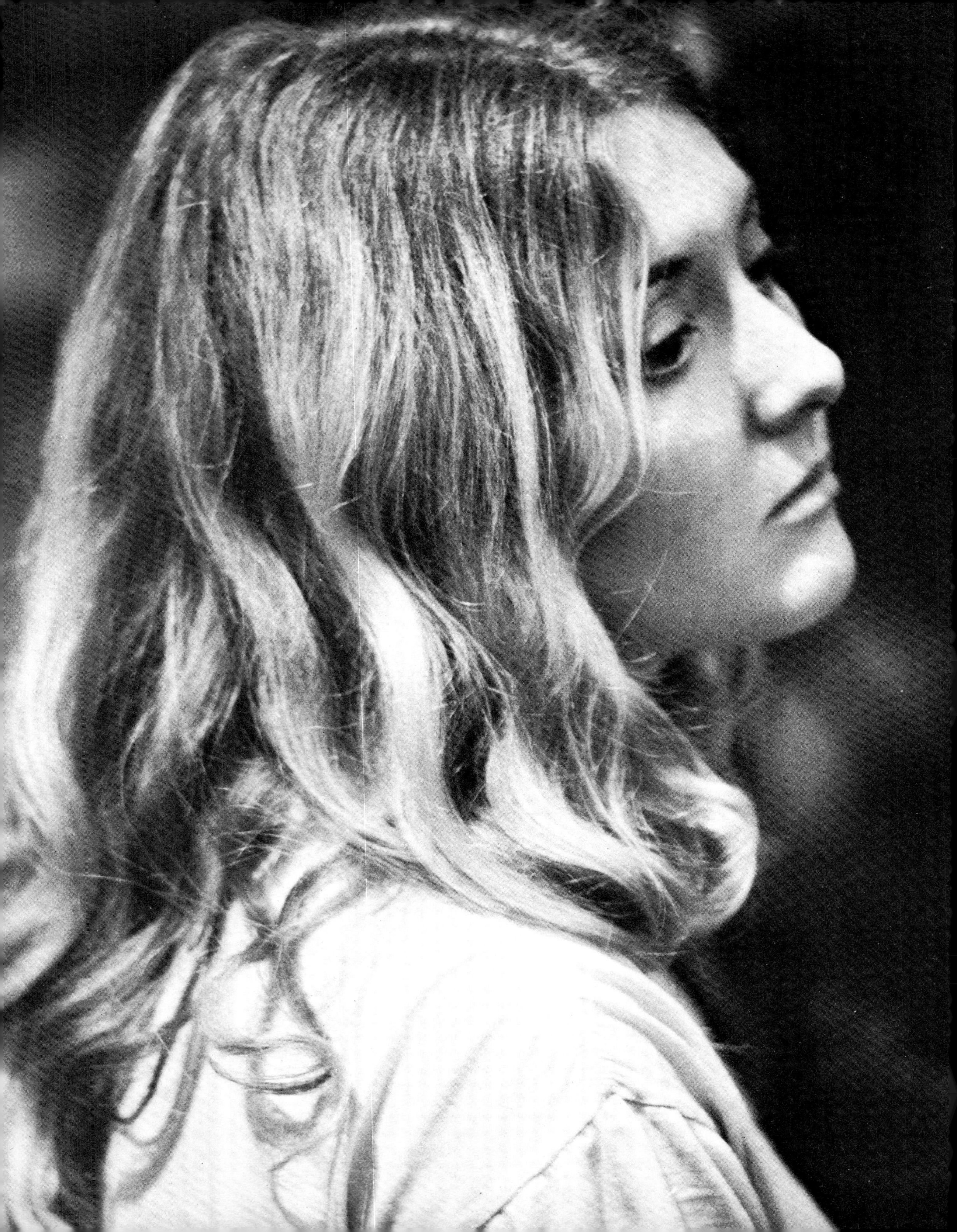

big ones. That blowing grass leads to shooting heroin, and all that. You've heard that all your life, right?

"But man, it's *true*. I have friends who say, 'I smoke pot but I'd never go to hard stuff.' And then I watch them disintegrate.

"You've heard the old argument over and over, 'one more won't hurt!' But it *will* hurt, it *will*. It gets your eyes off Jesus.

"I know we all get tired of hearing about hell and damnation all the time. But man, Jesus talked about hell more than all the prophets combined! We just have to give up on sin or we lose our tightness with God. That's just it."

The sermon is not a sermon and Chuck is not a preacher preaching. He goes on for almost an hour, conversationally, relating constantly, and no one looks like they want to leave.

Eventually it came time for the altar call. Chuck asked that heads bow, and that anyone who wanted to give their life to Christ should come up to the altar. He explained that he would pray with them, and then take them to a back office and talk to them for a while and let them go.

"If you have not yet given yourself to Christ, and you want to do that tonight, come on up to the altar," he said easily. "Just come on up right now."

A hundred kids—about equally divided, male and female, and between the ages of fifteen and nineteen—picked their way through the throng and stood at the altar.

After a short prayer, Chuck announced that the service was over and the huge crowd began to filter out into the patio. I asked if I could come along with the new converts. I had always been curious about what went on in those offices after people came forward for Christ. I had always harbored a suspicion—watching television ministries—that the people who were making their new spiritual persuasions public were hit up for extra money or something, once they were separated from the congregation. I always wondered why whatever happened back there had to happen privately.

In the rooms in back of the Chapel, Chuck took half the new converts and another young minister took the other half. Chuck closed the door and I looked around the room. There were about fifty young people. Some of them were wet-eyed, all of them had a look of real hope and anticipation. Chuck did what he said he'd do. He gave a short talk on how to remain a strong Christian.

"Read your Bible. If you don't have one, we'll give you one before you leave. But *read* it. And know that tonight is the first night of your whole spiritual life. That's pretty exciting, isn't it?" The group nodded with obvious enthusiasm.

"The second thing you got to do is pray. God is your Father. Talk to Him. Praise Him. And thank Him.

"Third thing to stay a strong Christian, you have to have fellowship—stay with brothers and sisters that are in the faith. You can be a Christian alone but it's not easy. We all need to support each other in our faith.

"Finally, witness. Go out and tell other people what Christ has done in your life. Share the good news.

"Now before you go, I want you to all say this prayer after me," Chuck said, and then he quietly spoke these words:

"Oh Heavenly Father, I know I am a sinner. Jesus forgive me for my sins. Make me right with God. Oh God, I accept You as my Master. Give me the strength to serve You. Help me to read the Bible, pray, keep fellowship with other Christians, and give witness to those who have not been born again. Jesus, I love you and I give my life to you. Just like you gave your life for me. Take me and use me. I ask it in your name. Amen."

We all recited the prayer with him, and when we looked up, there was this twenty-year-old guy, with long hair and wearing sneakers and jeans and a huge grin on his handsome face. "Welcome, Christians," he said. "Welcome brothers in Christ."

The next time I went to Calvary Chapel, a week later, Lonnie Frisbee was the minister. I had met him on my first trip to California and he was another person I wondered about. How had he been affected or changed by a year in which he had almost been made a media folk hero? More than that, he was getting to be legendary as an irresistible evangelist. It was widely accepted that Lonnie was responsible for tens of thousands of new converts in the southern California area. With that kind of attention, could he possibly be the same guy who a year ago said he could never get a swelled head because everything he did was for Jesus?

Well, that's one of those questions I suddenly wasn't asking myself any more. Lonnie's hair and his beard were a little longer, and maybe he had lost some weight. But

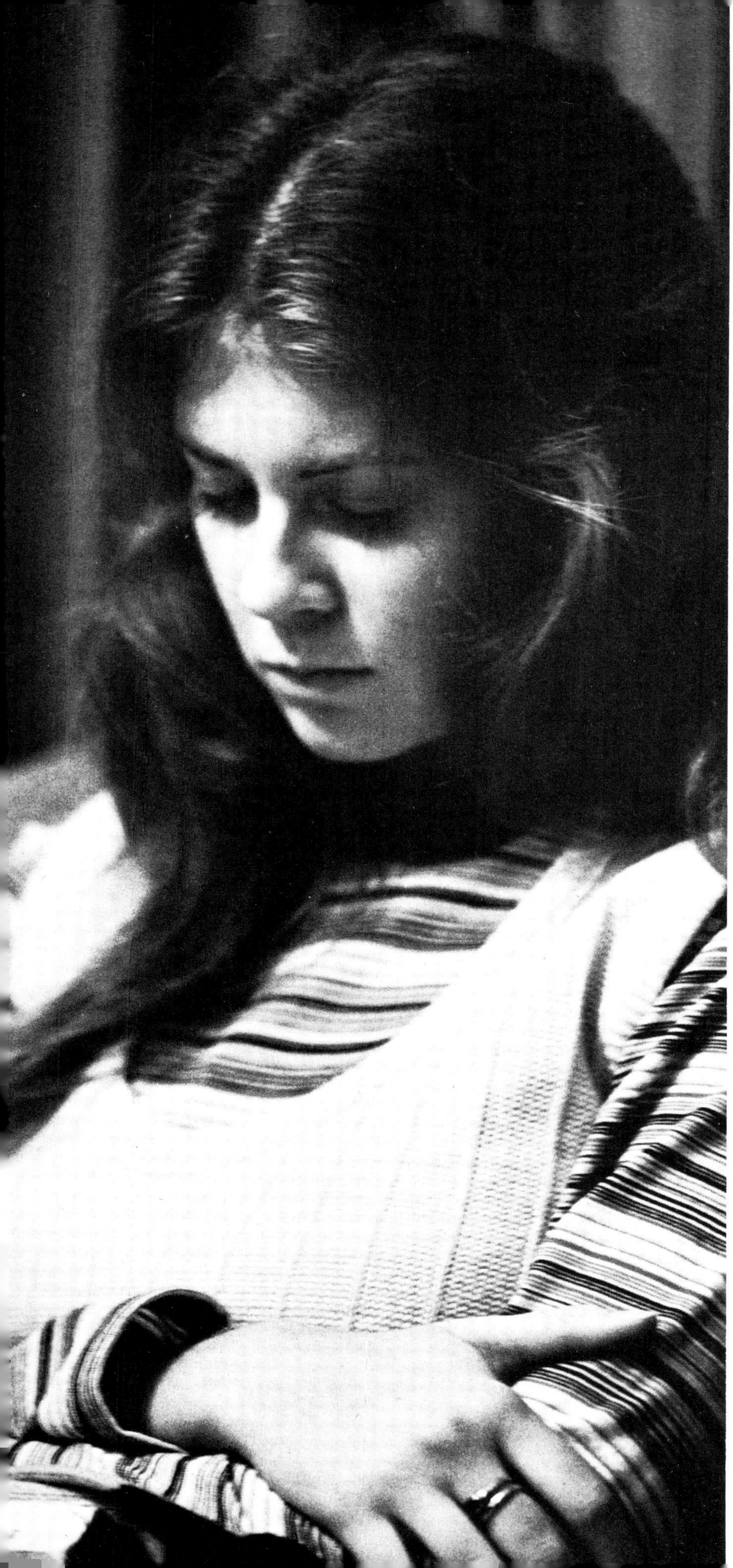

the incredible enthusiasm was still there, and the boundless energy that was apparently directed totally to serving his God, that was still there. I was getting more and more convinced that being saved was for a lot of people a pretty long-term proposition.

Of course Lonnie wasn't always like he is now. At fifteen, I was told, his leanings were toward commercial art and he had been offered a scholarship to the Art School in San Francisco. At seventeen, he was a dedicated drug-user and street person in the Haight. It was there that he met Ted Wise—one of the founders of the Haight storefront mission.

"He had a Christian background," Ted had told me earlier. "But his head was so bent out of shape from LSD that he had attached a whole lot of other junk to it.

"But we started talking to him at the mission, and he was really vitally interested in what we had to say. He came to live with us in our commune and saw the stability of our relationships. He began to study the Bible and pretty soon he decided to become a minister. He's a far-out guy."

Frisbee became a minister at age eighteen—which you can do in California just by getting a license—got married, and began his own Christian center called "The House of Miracles."

"But after a while, I felt that God wanted me to come down to southern California," Frisbee said. "I didn't know where I was going to go, but I was looking for a ministry I could join. It turned out that Chuck Smith at that time was praying for a hippie-type minister for the young people in the church. We just got together and it's been beautiful."

Calvary Chapel was packed as usual when I arrived the next week. Lonnie was conducting services in his usual way—relating to his congregation as Chuck Smith, Jr. had, but far less conversationally, far more emotionally. The range of his speaking voice covered a couple of octaves, and when he had a specifically urgent point to make, he could turn the volume way up.

"Calvary Chapel is nondenominational and I hope to heaven it always will be," Lonnie was saying. "There are something like 248 denominations in the world already. I don't think we need another . . .

"I really get insulted when someone calls me a Jesus

freak. I'm not a freak, I'm a *person*. I want to be called a Christian. I'm a member of the Body of Christ. And that's more important than being in any denomination.

"But there are new groups rising up here and there," Lonnie was warning. "They look and sometimes they talk like Christians. But there's something different about them. I've seen them down on the Strip in Hollywood. They had Bibles, and they were talking about Jesus, but there was something *wrong*. They were filthy dirty, for one thing. They seemed like they hadn't bathed for weeks. And they kept talking about repenting. The only thing you can do is repent. All you are is a sinner. Nothing about redemption."

Then Lonnie started talking about the so-called Children of God, a group of young Californians who frontiered an ultra-strict, totally anti-establishment Bible Camp called the "Soul Clinic" in Texas.

I had been told by a number of people that the Children of God were suspect. While their membership has swelled into the thousands as they sally forth from their camp to preach at beaches, campuses, and rock concerts, their motives were being questioned by a number of Christians.

"The Children of God are simply false prophets and the Bible warns in Revelations that we will have many false prophets in our midst," Lonnie shouted. "They say you have to give up all your possessions in order to accept Christ. I never saw anything in the Bible that says that. And they took kids away from their families and said that California was going to drop into the ocean. And that sure hasn't happened.

"You see you can be a false prophet even if you've been saved. How? Just by getting out of fellowship with Christ.

"There are going to be all kinds of phony cults cropping up and saying they are the real Jesus Movement. And there is one sure way to know the phonies."

Lonnie paused, and then shouted his sure way.

"EXCLUSIVISM!

"Any time someone says you have to come to *this* particular church, or dress *this* particular way, or sell all your property, or believe *their* particular way, you've got exclusivism. And that means you aren't part of the Body of Christ."

Then Lonnie moved into the part of the service which would call people to the altar. I couldn't help thinking, how many times has he done this—maybe several times a week for several years? His mind must

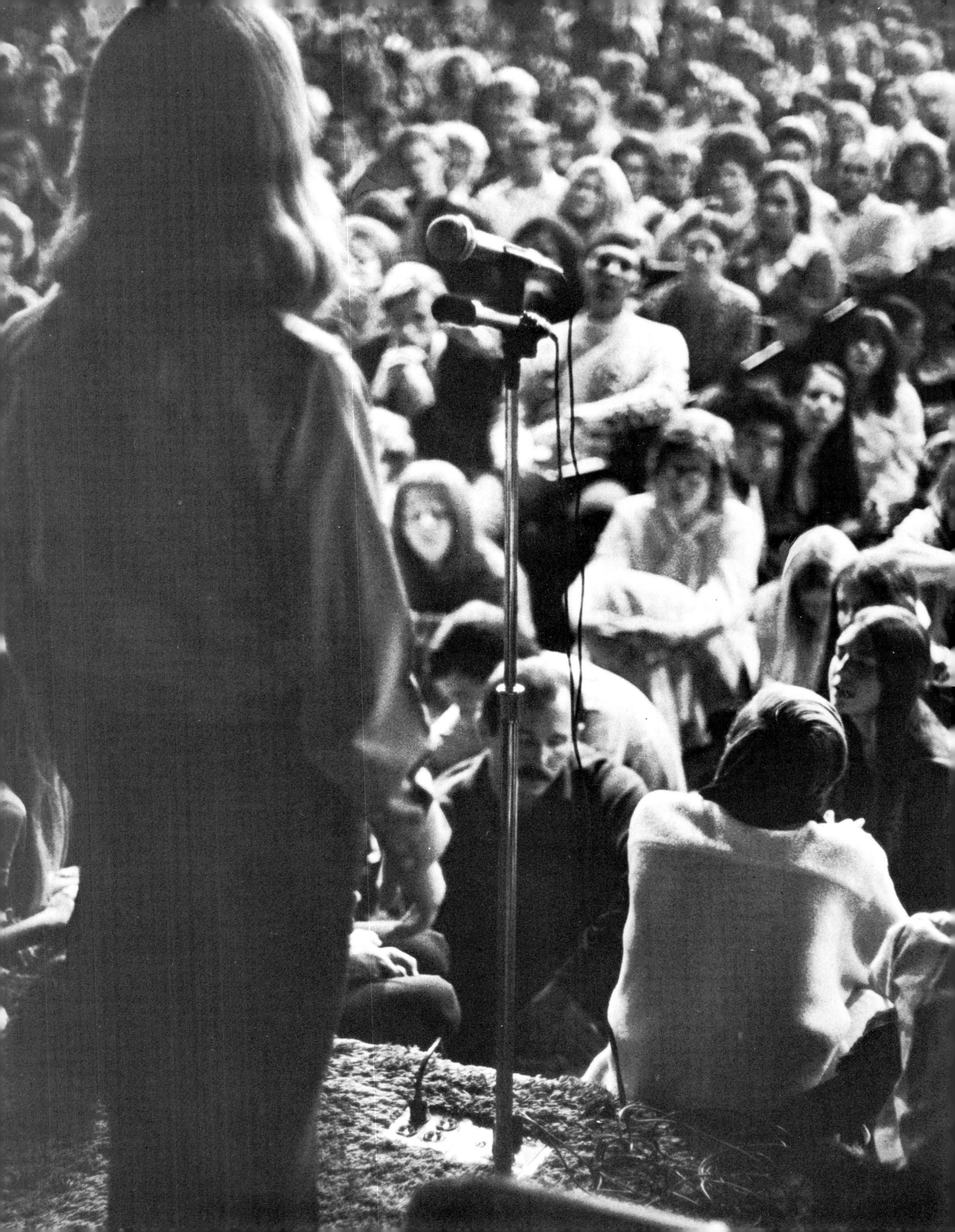

sometimes wander. I wondered if he didn't sometimes just wish he were somewhere else, doing something else.

But I could never tell that by his call. His voice was lyrical and persuasive—almost hypnotizing. "There is a new life Jesus has for you tonight. It begins the moment you ask him into your heart.

"Some of you have been doing your own thing—having your own bag. Well you're going to be stuck holding the bag when Jesus comes. And he is coming back soon. So accept Jesus. He's speaking to you right now. Just listen. You can hear him. Come up here now. I know there are lots of you who want to accept Jesus tonight. Just come right up here. Jesus is waiting."

Dozens of young people were rising out of their seats and moving toward the front of the chapel. Close to where I was standing, a young man slowly rose to his feet and walked forward. Next to him a petite redhead, obviously his girl friend, clenched both her fists in delight and closed her eyes. "Oh thank you Jesus," she murmured, barely able to contain her happiness. "Oh thank you, sweet, precious Jesus."

Lonnie was still calling. "I know there are some more of you out there who feel the Spirit moving inside you. Some of you older people. Here are your children ready to commit their lives to Jesus Christ. Are you strong enough to make that commitment?"

A gray-haired lady in the back of the church took off her glasses, stood up and walked with a sort of regal dignity toward the altar.

"Oh praise God!" many of the congregation called out, and they applauded.

When all the new converts had reached the front of the church, Lonnie asked the congregation to bow their heads in prayer. The room suddenly became motionless, soundless. Everyone was praying silently, or at least thinking quietly, and the church seemed frozen in time.

Then there grew a gradual noise—the slight whir of a car engine, a car coming up the road, closer and closer, and louder and louder until it passed directly in front of the church, and someone yelled from the front window, "Jesus is dead!"

It shattered the moment like glass, but immediately a girl sitting near me stood and turned toward the direction of the disappearing car and shouted at the top of her voice, "BULLSHIT!"

The silence that was immediately re-established was

even more total than it had been before. But after a few moments, it was quietly broken again as the girl who offered the impulsive rejoinder began sobbing, her hands covering her face.

"I don't know what made me do that," she said shaking her head from side to side. "I really don't know why I had to go and do that."

Two friends came over to comfort her and one, a tall girl who looked to be in her early twenties said, loud enough for everyone in the chapel to hear, "I've always been taught that if it's in your heart to say, you should say it. I don't think you did anything wrong."

The congregation gratefully amened, and the tension was broken.

The service was brought to an end with a hymn, and then Lonnie led the dozens of new converts back to the church offices.

If Lonnie Frisbee and Chuck Smith, Jr. and Sr., were Army recruiters, I was thinking, there wouldn't be many civilians.

Once each month, the ministers of Calvary Chapel hold a massive baptism in a gently rounded harbor area in Newport Beach. These baptisms are, according to Chuck Smith, more outward signs than sacraments.

"A lot of these kids were baptized by their parents when they were infants," Smith said. "But they want to go through it again. They want to make it *their* decision."

At the Baptisms I attended, hundreds of people—some there for the fellowship, some from curiosity—stood and sat in the amphitheater-like rock wall that surrounded three sides of the harbor. Hundreds more were down on the sand by the water.

Before the Baptisms began, a young couple were married by Chuck Smith at the water's edge. They had been living together for months, they told me, but then together accepted Christ and decided to make it legal and Christian.

The wedding ceremony itself was not an unusual one. Smith stood with his back to the water and had the couple recite the standard vows. When it came time to exchange rings, he said "these rings are a symbol of God's love. They have no beginning and no end—they just go on and on."

The people surrounding the ceremony laughed when

Smith said that, a laugh of pleasant appreciation, as if they were all sharing a secret joke about God's love.

"And now according to the power invested in me by the state of California," Smith concluded, "I now pronounce you man and wife."

The young couple embraced and then turned around to see the audience that had now grown to over a thousand and were witnesses to their wedding.

"Oh wow," the groom said, obviously pleased and astonished at the multitude of uninvited guests.

Then, almost spontaneously, the crowd broke into a standard hymn, "Highway to Heaven," and the Baptisms were about to begin.

"This water represents the grave," Smith said, sweeping his hand behind him at the vast Pacific. "Those of you who are being baptized today will have all your past buried in that grave. Open your heart and let God's spirit descend upon you. In this Baptism, you identify with Jesus in his death, burial, and new life."

Dozens of the new Christians began moving toward the water, some stripping down to bathing suits, others just standing by the shore fully dressed. The three ministers

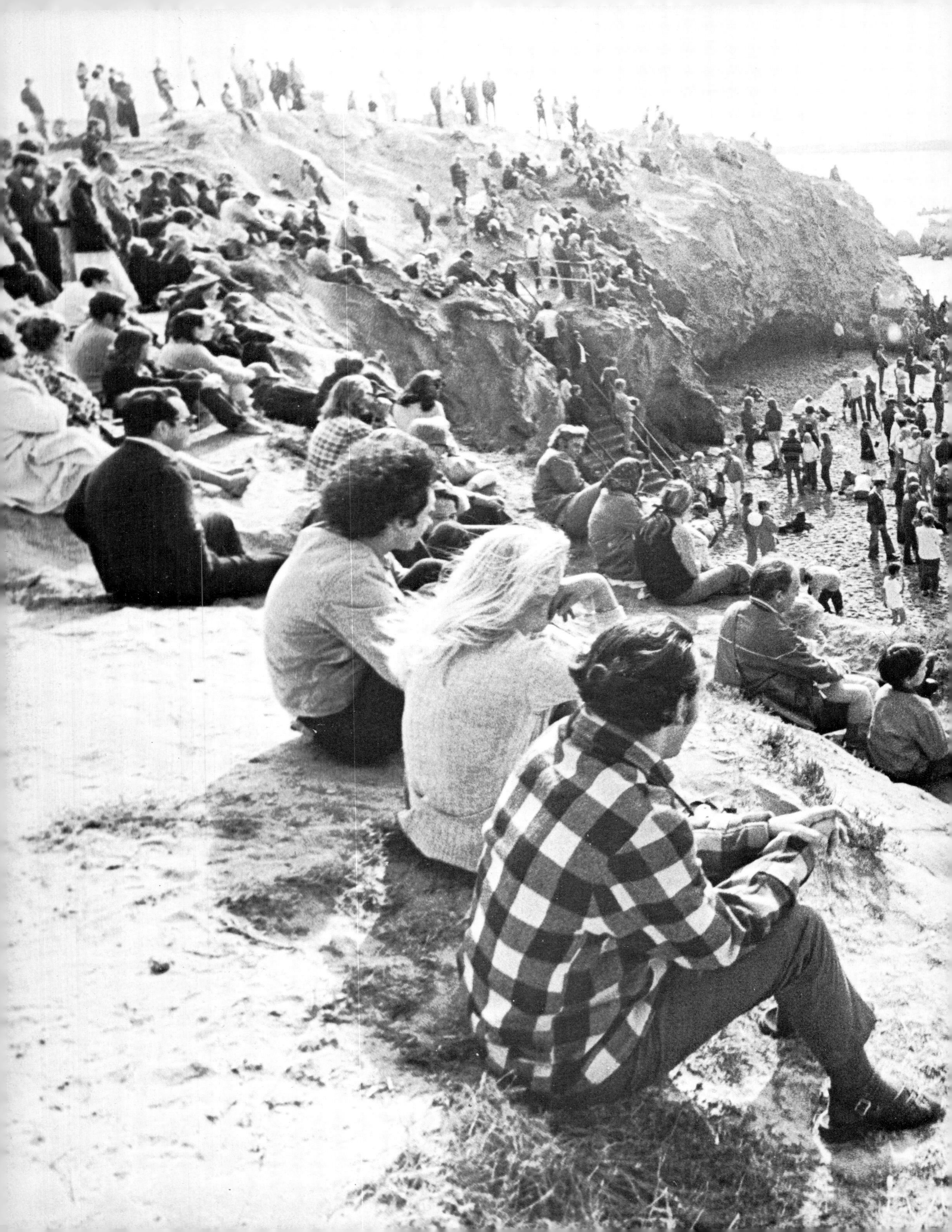

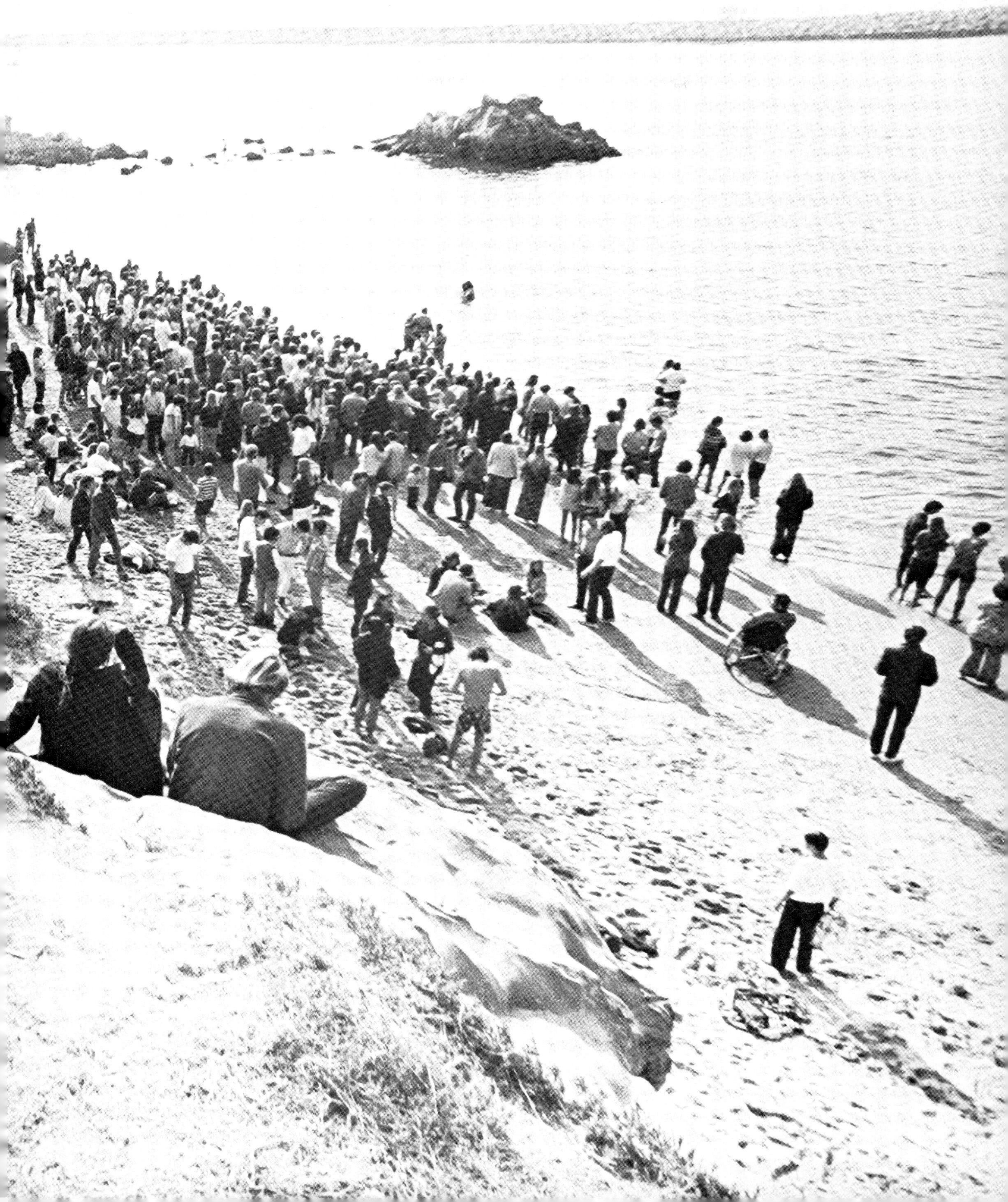

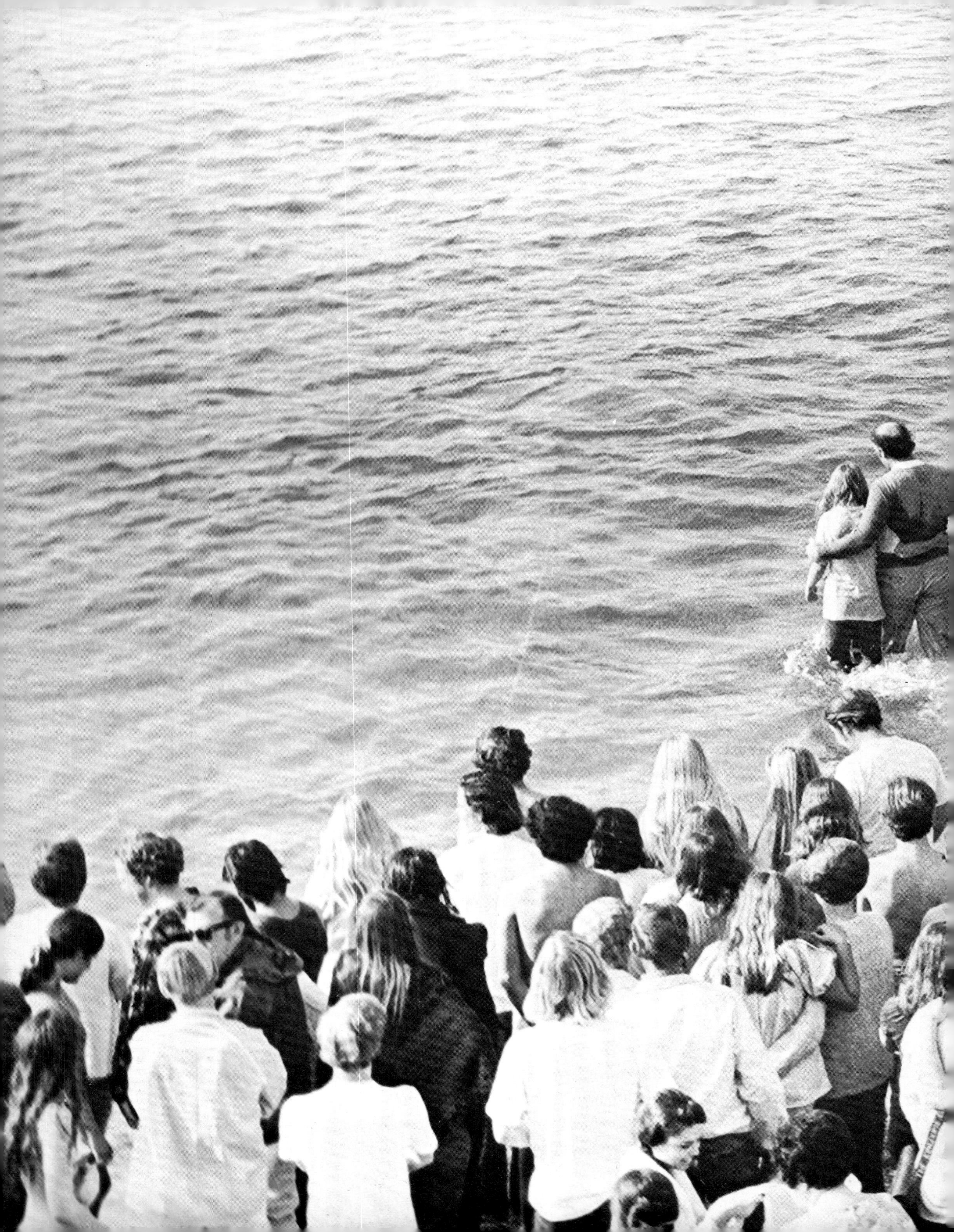

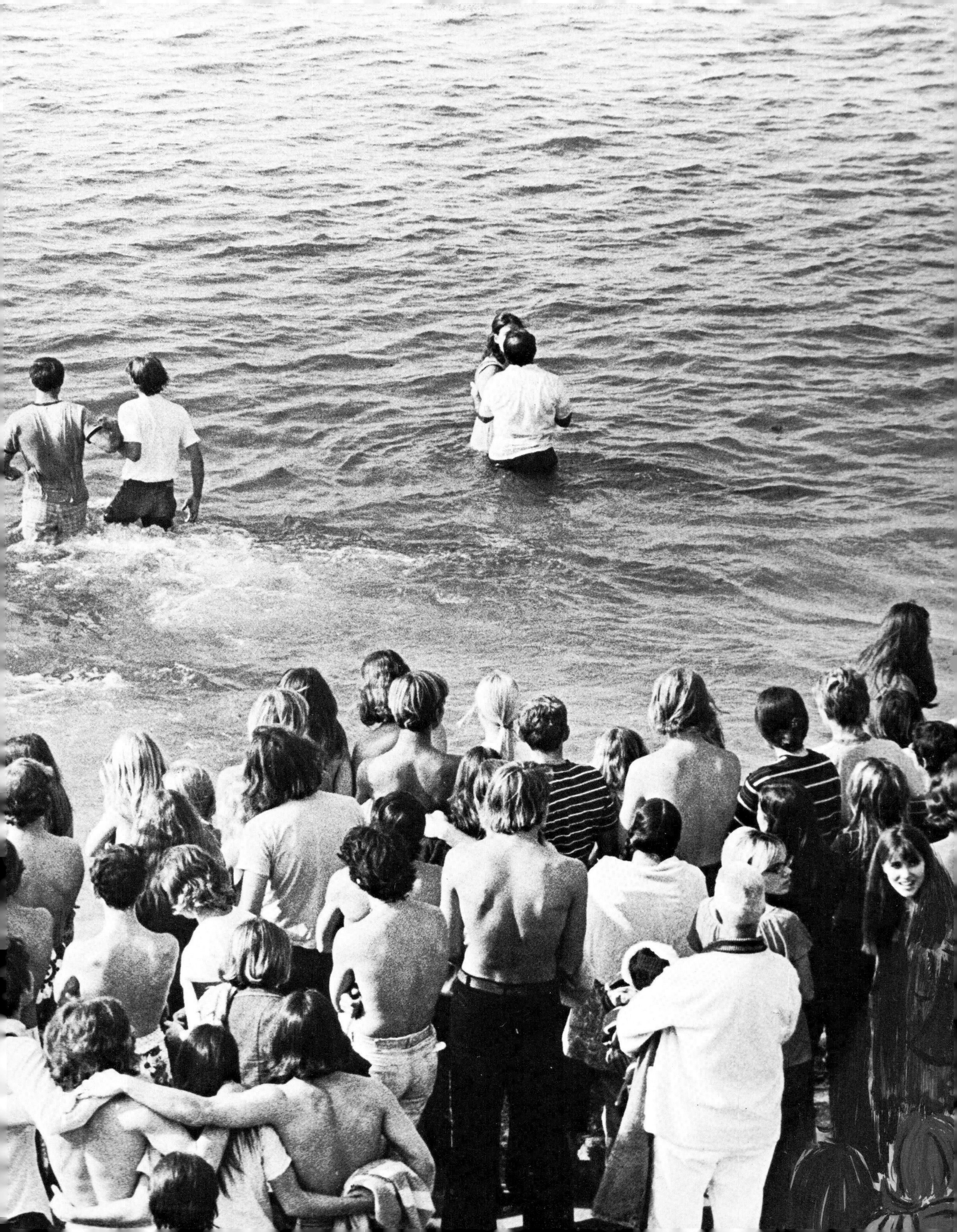

led the young people out into the water, each minister taking one convert at a time. They would wade to water about waist deep, pray for a moment, and then the minister would place his hand over the nose and mouth of the convert and dip him backward for a brief second of total immersion.

Then, dripping and shivering and looking positively other-worldly, the newly baptized would be led back to the shore where they were greeted by friends. And on that shore, everyone was a friend. There was hugging, uninhibited joy, and welcoming embraces.

As a total scene, it was as if one overpowering cone of happiness was emanating from that sheltered beach area, a palpable aura of oneness, gladness swelling from the water and enveloping the cove.

And as I walked around the beach, looking and listening, I saw dozens of miniature dramas that contributed to the giant scenario of love.

One young man came in from the water and walked over to where to his wife was standing, holding their small child in her arms. "Now, we begin," he said. "Oh thank you," she said and tears of happiness poured down her face.

A heavyset youth, wedged in a wheelchair that had held him since he was old enough to sit, was rolled to the edge of the water where three of his friends lifted his paralyzed body and helped Smith carry him into the water.

Some of the newly baptized walked off alone for moments of prayer when they came out of the water. They would kneel in a corner of the rocks and move their lips silently in words of obvious thanksgiving, and then rise and join the others.

Others, as they were led out of the water, were shouting. It was an exhilaration of release, as if some terrible burden had just been lifted from them, and they couldn't wait to get back on shore and tell people about it.

One tow-headed youngster about twelve years old was led out of the water with his small hand lost in Chuck Smith's. He was handed over to his mother who was waiting for him with a towel. "Is that what you wanted to come down here for?" she asked, more perplexed than disturbed. "Was that all?" He said nothing, and the two walked up the rocks to a waiting station wagon above.

All around the beach, small groups were forming to pray, or to sing, or just to talk. "I was just reading in

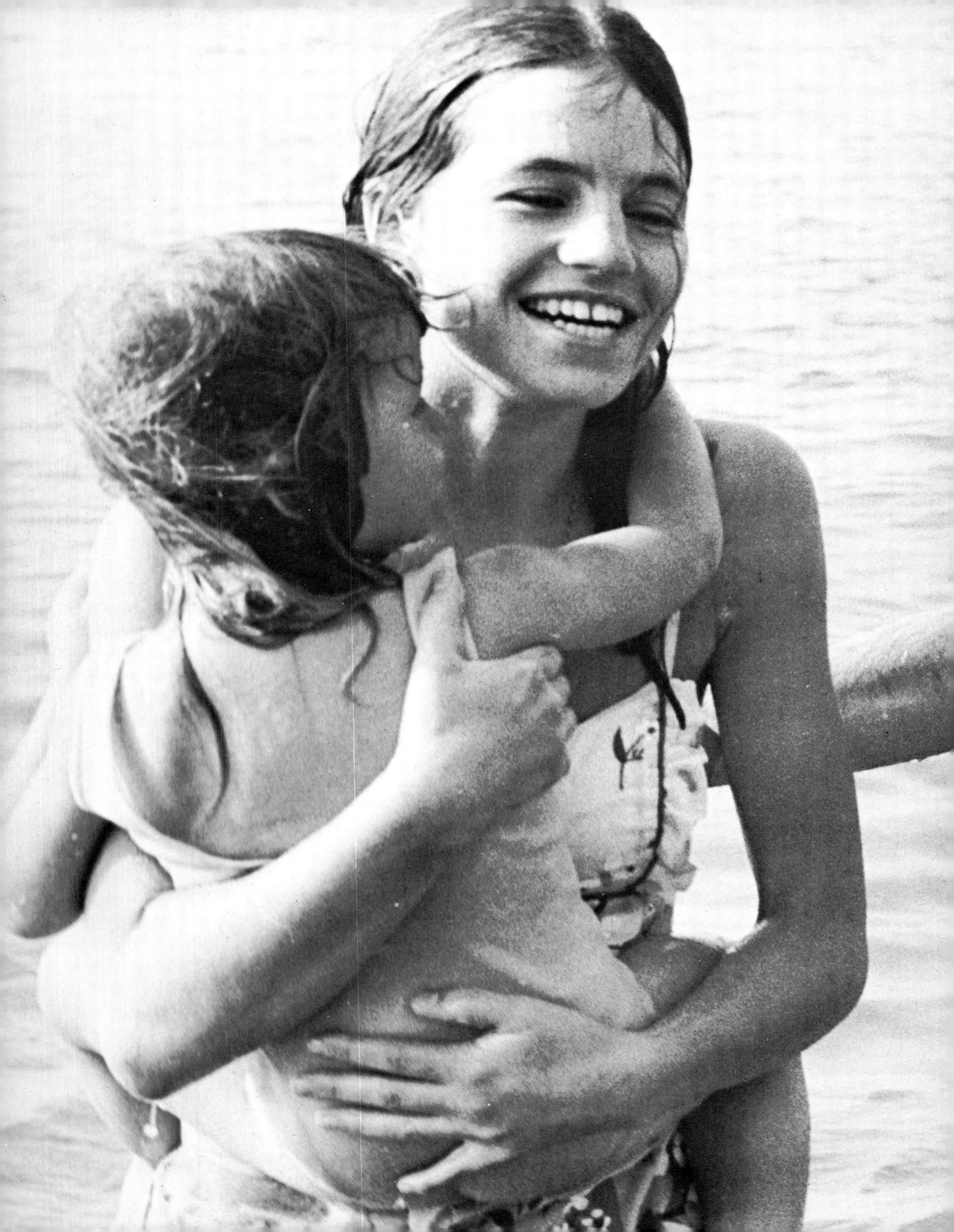

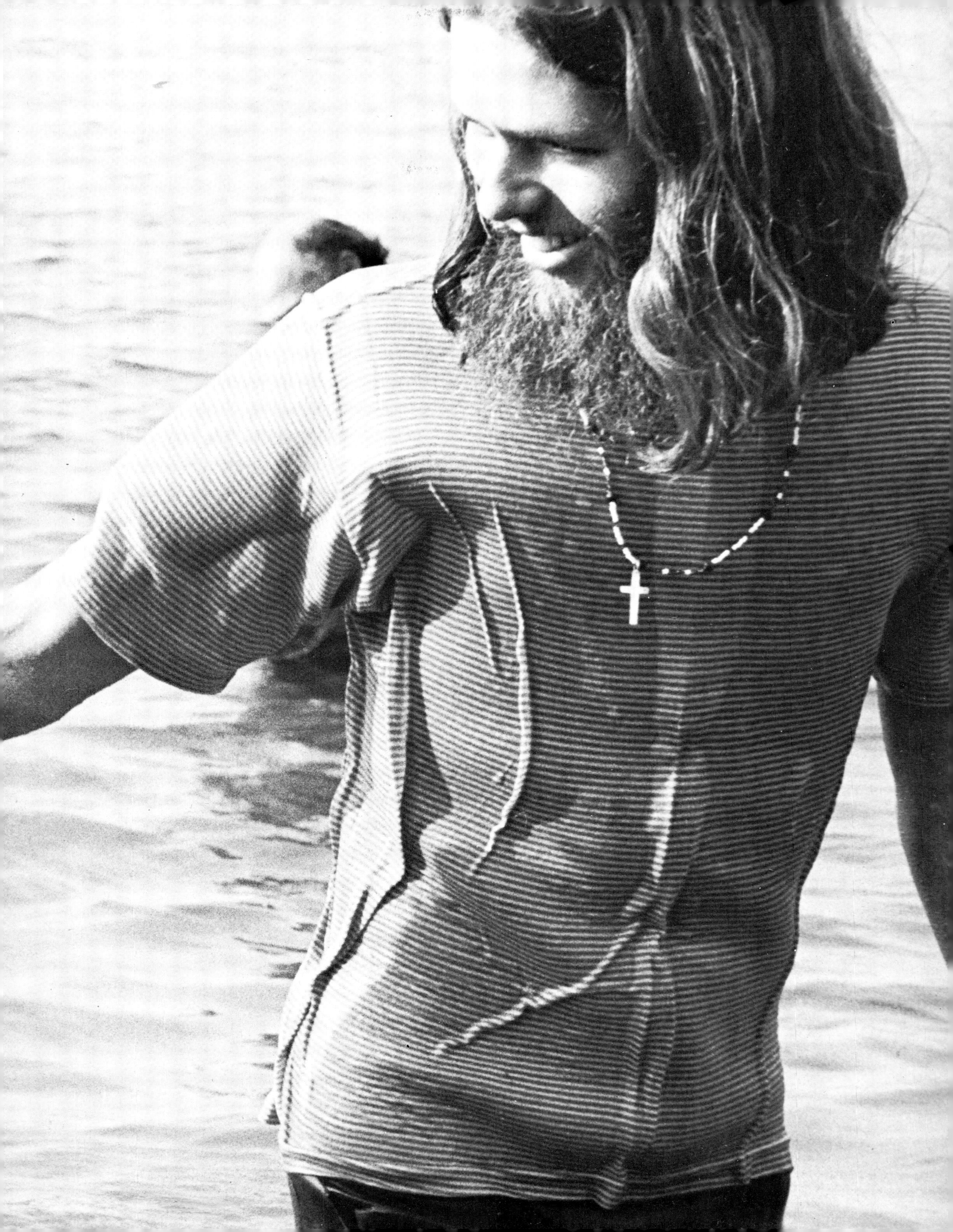

Ephesians..." I heard a guy say, just like you'd hear someone at a cocktail party say, "Well according to *Fortune* last week...." I accidentally stepped on a fellow's bare foot, and he apologized to me. That's what kind of crowd it was.

I saw a young girl being led out of the water and she stopped me cold. I had never seen a face like hers in my life—thin wet hair surrounding a face that radiated utter bliss. When she reached shore, half a dozen of her friends crowded around to embrace her—young men and women who obviously wanted to take very special care of this frail and lovely child.

"Who is she?" I asked a girl who was standing a few feet away, beaming at the hugging that was going on.

"Her name is René," I was told. "Three weeks ago, she wandered into Miracle House—that's a drug help center up in Silverado. She was stoned and scared. You wouldn't have known it was the same person three weeks ago."

When the embraces were finally over, I asked René if we could go somewhere and talk. She still looked slightly stunned and very ecstatic, and she nodded her head. We went off to a corner in the rock formation.

"They tell me you were in pretty funny shape not long ago."

"Yea. I'd been smoking a lot of joints, and my boy friend had just kicked me out of the house. I didn't know what I was doing or where I was going. I don't know what made me go into Miracle House. I was just standing in front of it and all of a sudden I was inside.

"And that very day, I asked Jesus to come into my heart, and he's been with me ever since."

"How long do you think it will last," I said.

"Oh, it's going to last forever. There isn't anything else."

"You look kind of cold," I said. She was shivering, clutching a towel around her thin shoulders. The temperature was barely in the sixties.

"I'm not cold. I'm filled with the Holy Spirit."

"You also look very beautiful."

"You see the Lord in me."

"And you also look a little stoned."

"I *am* stoned," she said breathlessly. "I'm stoned on Jesus. Drugs are a down, but this is the most incredible up in the world. I feel like I'm floating all the time, with Jesus."

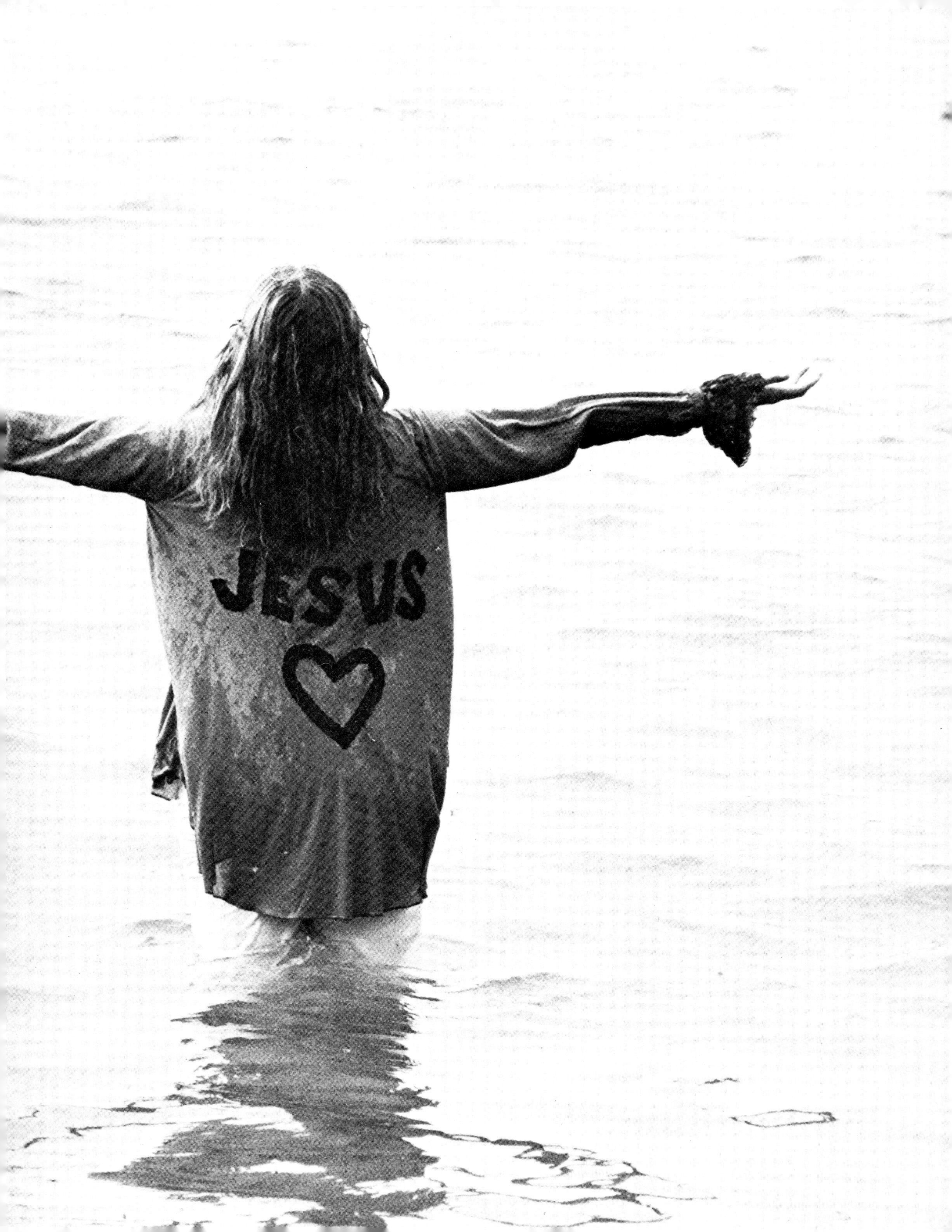
JESUS

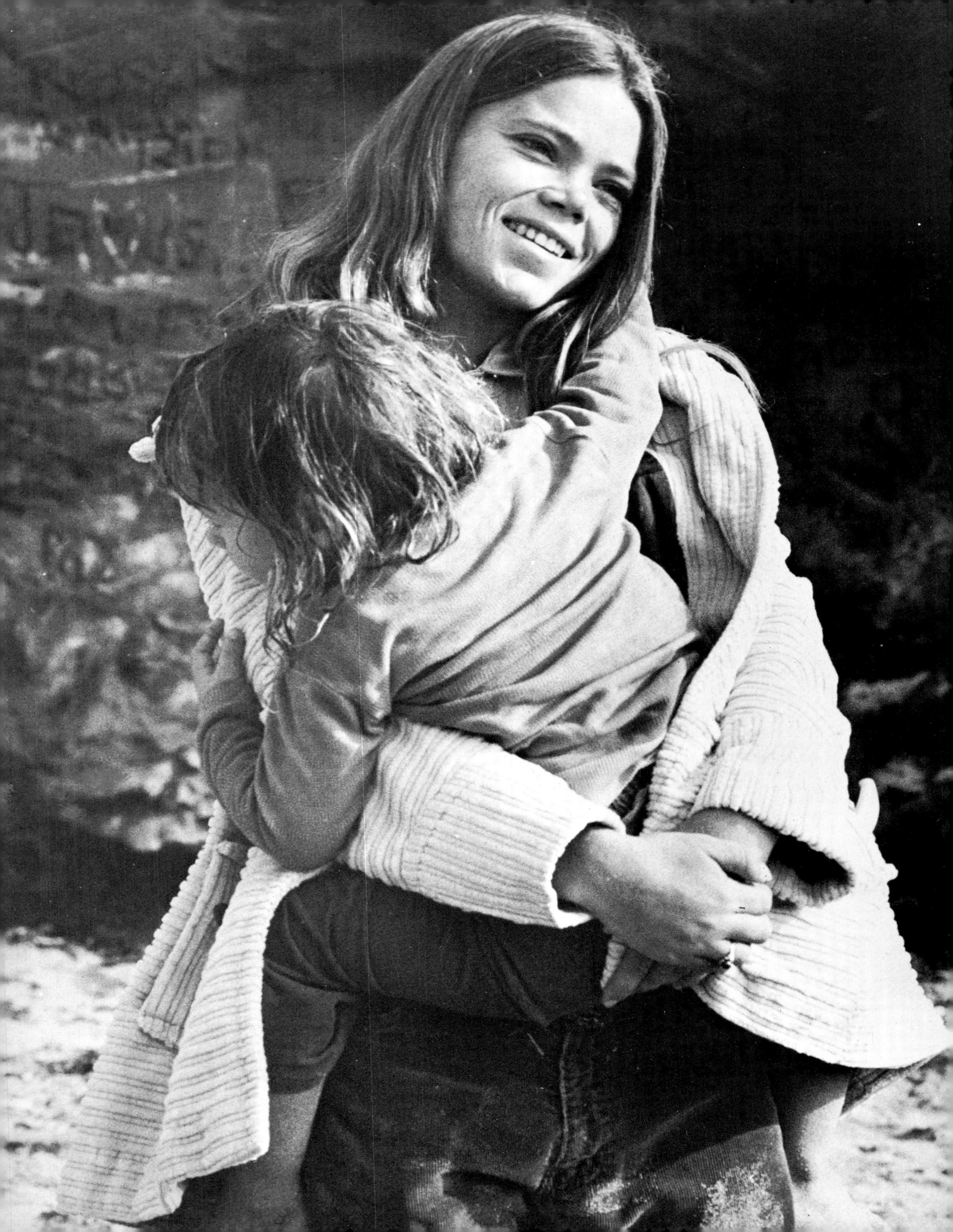

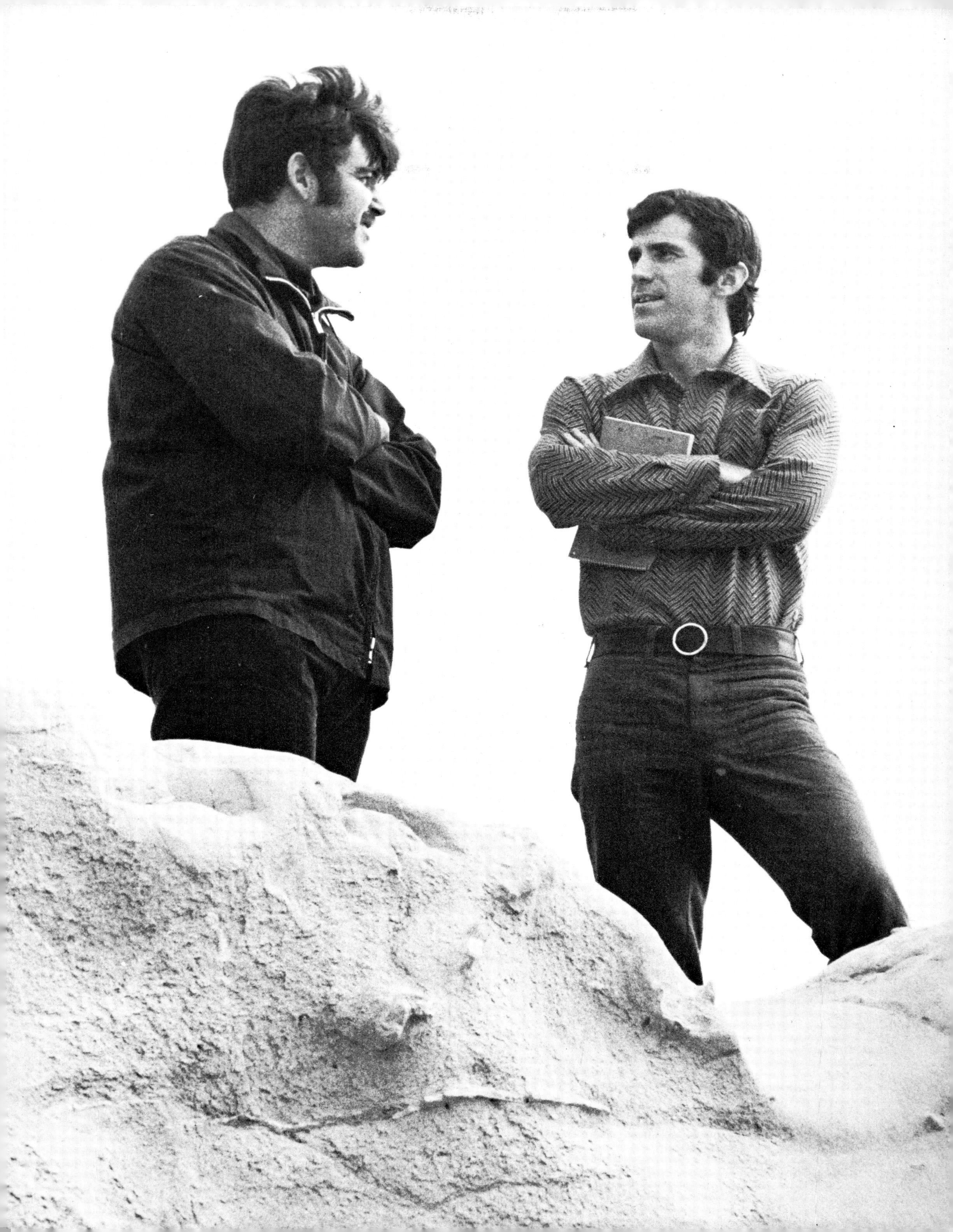

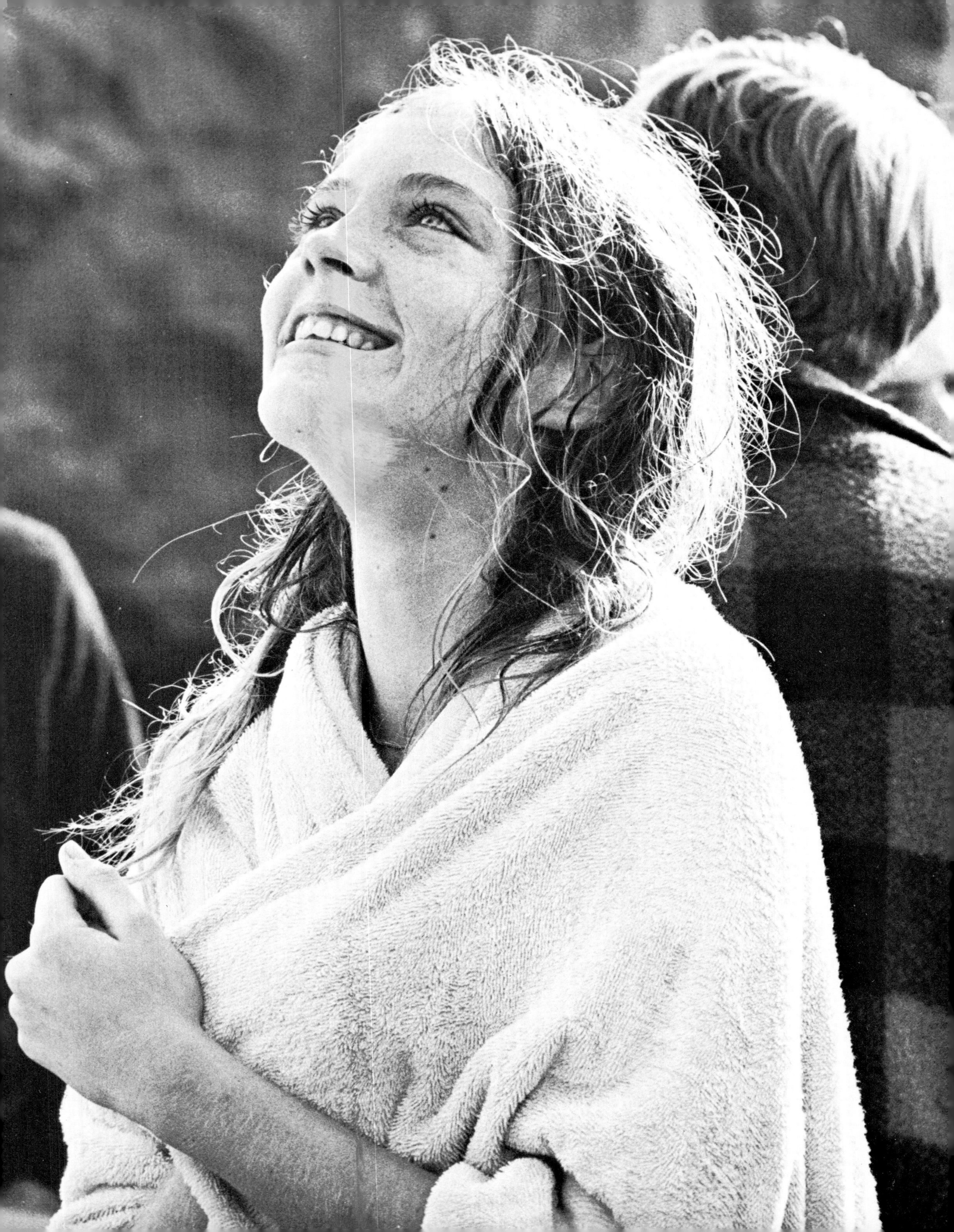

"They say he's coming soon," I said. I was making conversation. I just didn't want to leave this radiant child for a moment.

"Yes, He will come back. He's coming very soon," René said. "It will be the time of the Rapture. He will take the people who have accepted him as personal savior. We will be raptured."

"What's 'raptured'?" I asked. It was a word I'd heard Christians use from time to time, but I never really understood what it was supposed to mean.

"That's when Jesus calls his chosen people—all of us who have accepted him—and no matter what we are doing at that moment, he takes us right up into Heaven. Just like that, in a flash. In that second, we will all be with him in heaven. How about you, have you accepted Jesus as your personal Lord and Savior?"

"That's a question I get asked a lot," I said. "But thanks for talking to me, René. I think your friends are waiting for you over there. But, really, thanks for sharing with me. I hope this is the most important day of your life."

One of the extensions of Calvary Chapel are communal houses—homes given over to the church for little or no money which are turned into Christian communes—run and disciplined by an elder and centered around prayer and Christian fellowship.

Calvary has dozens of such houses throughout the western seaboard. "We can't open them fast enough," Chuck Smith said. "They just get filled up with kids and then someone will move out to open another one, and on and on it goes."

I visited one such house in Orange called the "Mansion Messiah," then headed by thirty-year-old Ed Smith, an amiable and comparatively new Christian who was both elder of the house and a $25,000-a-year fiber glass salesman.

"It took me twenty-nine years to accept Christ," Smith told me smiling. "But after all that argument, I finally let him into my life. I think you could say it was one of my smarter moves."

And here that thing was happening to me again. Smith looked and talked like a guy who I could go and have a beer with, and we could talk about football or presidential primaries. Like George Wakeling and Steve Kosca at Melodyland, here was a guy who hadn't faced any climactic terror or trouble that forced him to wrap himself in a religion. He wasn't coming off drugs and he wasn't highly emotional or hyperactive. He was just an awfully nice fellow I really liked on sight, who got hit inexplicably by religion.

"Tell me about the house," I said.

"Well, the objective is to take young people who are unsettled in the world and give them a foundation by establishing them in the word of God.

"We get all kinds here, all walks of life. The thing they have in common is that they all have tried to fill that void in their heart—find some false substitute for God. It can be anything from drugs to alcohol, to excessive recreation, to sex, to stuffing Oreos after supper—anything to fill up the hole."

"And it doesn't work," I said.

"Of course it doesn't work. There's only one thing that does. Only one answer.

"Now I'm not saying our house is an easy place for someone to live in. It's great for spiritual growth, but pretty hard on the desires of the flesh. People might want a nice roomy apartment with comfort and privacy, and this house doesn't afford any of those things."

The Mansion Messiah—like most Christian houses—is self-supporting. The young people who come to the house are told they are going to have to work. If they are runaways and under age, they are told they must get permission from their parents before they can come to live. And the livin' ain't easy.

"We expect everyone to get up at the same time," Smith said. "We get up at six a.m. and eat breakfast at seven a.m. We all go to bed at approximately ten p.m. We all eat at the same time in the evening.

"When someone wants to go someplace, they have to ask and check out. Part of the reason for this is that we are a working body, a working ministry. If we don't know where the twenty-five to forty people living here are, we're not going to be worth much. We stick close together. No one's off doing his own thing. Kids give up a lot to come and serve God in a house like this.

"I used to find my substitute for God in drinking, many nights a week. I was becoming an up-and-coming young executive salesman. I was doing all the proper things, and that meant martinis at eleven-thirty in the morning until about two the following morning.

"One day, one of my customers told me he was going to show me what I was missing in life. I thought he was kind of a kook. But we talked and talked, and eventually I accepted Jesus Christ as my Lord and Savior. He's a lot better than any high I've ever had off liquor."

The inhabitants of Mansion Messiah are strictly segregated. The girls live upstairs and the boys live downstairs, and the only reason anyone has for being in anyone else's room is to clean it up.

If a girl in the house wants to date someone outside who is not a Christian, Smith tells her to go ahead. "But I also encourage her to take along a brother from the house, and her Bible."

With rules like that, I expected to meet a pretty somber group when I was invited to a potluck supper at the Mansion Messiah.

Instead I found a bunch of kids walking around in what seemed like a euphoric, stoned state—only these kids were glowing. I was sure that if I turned off all the lights, I'd still be able to see their faces.

The house was filled to over capacity for this open dinner. Everyone was greeted at the door by a house member who said cheerfully, "Do you know Jesus Christ as your personal savior?" The password was "yes" or "no," it didn't make much difference. The Christians were welcomed as brothers; the heathens were welcomed as friends.

The supper was delicious—bowls and bowls of spaghetti, rice, banana bread, chicken casserole, beef stew—all made at the house with obviously far more expertise than expense.

While I was eating, I got into a conversation with a sixteen-year-old named Margie who lived at home with her mother but who came to the Mansion for occasional fellowship. So, I found out, did her mother.

"At first, it was pretty bad. She and I were growing further and further apart—fighting, and then not even talking. I was into grass a lot, and I guess she knew it but didn't know what to say to me about it.

"Then one day a friend of mine invited me to this Bible song festival and I went along just because I didn't have anything better to do. A girl there told me that I should open my heart to Jesus and I'd find great happiness. I said not me—I could never get into that kind of stuff.

"But that night I was lying in bed and I said, 'Jesus, I'm not even sure if you exist. But if you do, I'm opening my heart to you. Or at least that's what I'm trying to do. So if you're there, I'm open.'

"That's all I did. Then I fell asleep and the next morning I woke up filled with this incredible good feeling."

As Margie was talking, she could hardly sit still. She was bouncy, and gestured extravagantly. "I told my mother, and she just hugged me, and we're just so close now. It's just so great! Some of my friends hassle me a little, but I tell them, you just don't know what you're missing."

Many of the conversions related to me were that simple: a prayer—a person saying "God, if you're up there, please listen," and then that indescribable new emotional birth. But I was thinking as I heard these stories that that kind of changeover can't be sustained without support. The suddenness and the overpowering feeling of accepting Jesus Christ as the most important real entity in one's life has to have some kind of spiritual booster shots. Or at least, so it seemed to me.

And in the California Jesus Movement, those clinics for out-patient new-believer support are abundant. They come in the expected form—mid-week church services and extensive Bible studies. But they also can be found in something new in American youth revivals—religious coffeehouses.

In Southern California alone, there are dozens of them, named for unabashed youth appeal: "Soul Hut," "Fire Escape," "His Place," and "Thy Brother's House." Their big business is on Friday and Saturday nights, and they have very definitely dislodged a number of discothèques—becoming the teenagers' habitual weekend hangouts. The entertainment is a sermon by the resident minister, group hymns, mass praying in tongues and a constant, supportive reaffirmation of Christian fellowship.

They are coffeehouses looking the way one would expect a California coffeehouse to look—pillows on the floor, guitarist on a makeshift stage, coffee and light refreshments served in the back. But the entertainment is built upon group participation. New and old hymns are sung by everyone, arms interlocked and all the bodies swaying to the cadence.

Then, the most informal of altar calls is delivered: "Anyone need praying tonight?" a young leader will ask. And somebody will. And the praying will begin—everyone joins and the matter of the moment is to bring Jesus into the room directly upon that one person.

"Dear Lord, dear sweet Jesus, help this brother tonight..." on and on into the night. The parents and police reluctantly allow that it keeps the kids off the street. But it does more than that. It keeps them tight with their fellow believers—on weekends, when the temptations of "the world" are leering on every street corner, the Christian coffeehouses are jumping with Jesus talk.

"Have you ever noticed how kids know all the lyrics of the popular rock songs?" Chuck Smith said one time. "It's because groups like the Rolling Stones have been talking directly to the kids, talking through the words of their songs. Now if you ask a kid to repeat a few lines of the songs he used to sing in the choir, he'd give you a blank stare. That music hasn't related to them at all. It's been a bore.

"Now when they hear songs about Jesus with the same kind of beat and background as rock, or country music, the kids are going to start picking up on the lyrics. They're going to start listening. They're coming to realize that Jesus Christ is a person to whom they can relate in a modern-day setting."

If the group at the U.S.C. College auditorium that night for the Jesus Music concert was any example, Chuck Smith's assessment of the new Christian music was accurate to the extreme.

The auditorium was jammed with young people—over a thousand crammed into the bleachers and huddled on the floor. The floodlighted platform was draped with a latticework of electrical wires and jammed with amplifiers. It could very well have been a stage to frame the Grateful Dead or Jefferson Airplane, and the crowd could very easily be like the multi-colored groupies that used to swell the insides of Fillmores East and West.

The thing I was finding out more and more, was that the trappings of those caught up in the Jesus Movement were not changed. Just their substance, their thinking took on a new look.

When the first band ambled onto the stage, their regalia was the uniform of the day. Striped pants, sandals, modishly regulated hair, leather vests, and totally electric music—including an electric fiddle. The group was called "Love Song" and their sound was modern Nashville. Their reception was loud and enthusiastic.

"We're not talking and singing about any religion or denomination or once-every-Sunday trip," said the 24-year-old leader of the group. "We're talking about the real Body of Christ, and if you feel it with us, sing along:

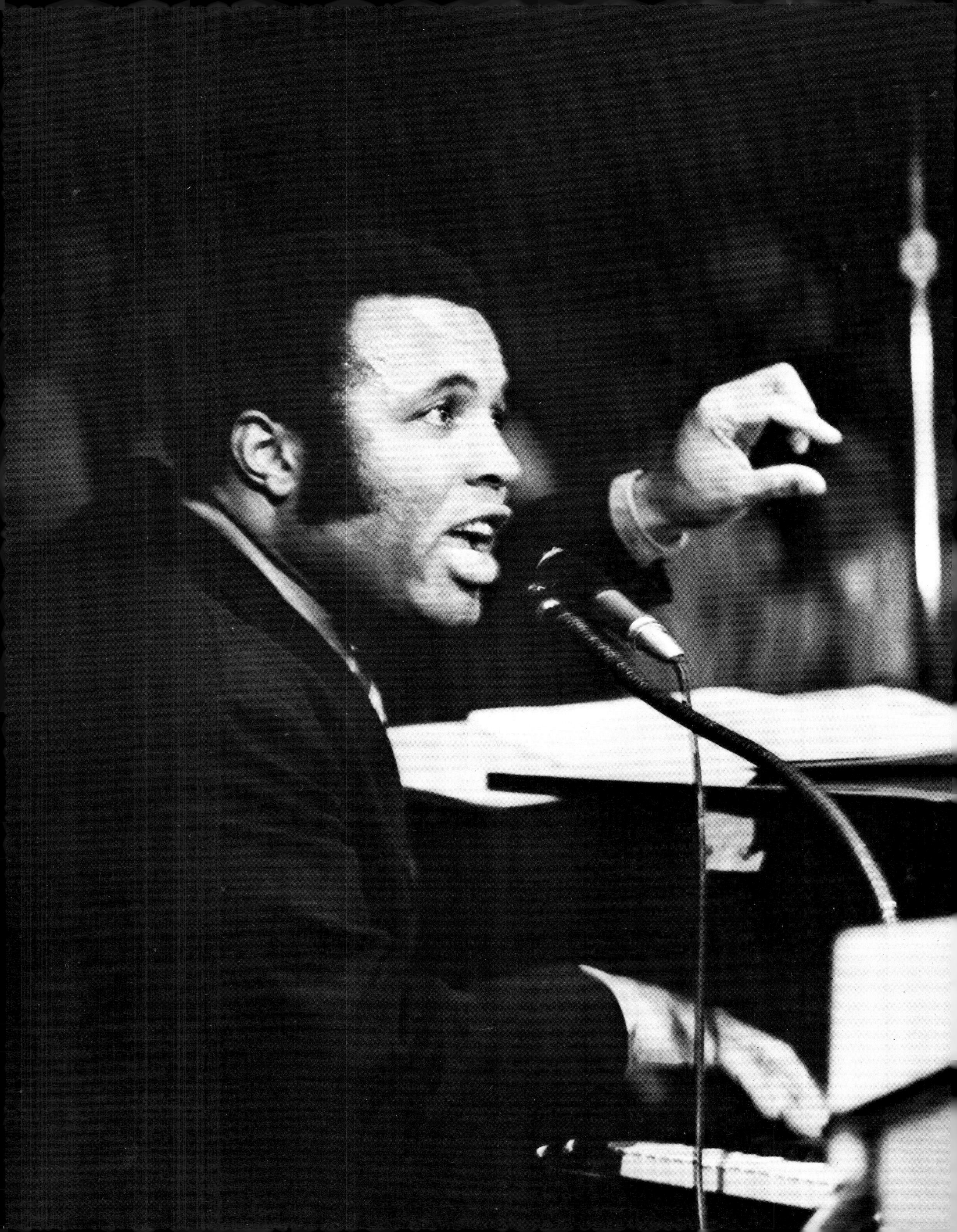

Since I opened up,
Opened up the door,
I can't think of anything
But you any more.
Since I opened up,
Opened up the door,
Jesus is the only one
Who I am living for.

And the crowd did sing along, clapping their hands and swaying back and forth to the loud, hoedown sound.

The next group on stage was André Crouch and the Disciples, and their reception was almost deafening. The group was black—one of the few groups of blacks I had seen at any time while looking at the Movement in California—and Crouch himself was a big, authoritative man whose piano was hot soul.

It's just like walking in the sunshine
After a long and dreary day.
I have a satisfied feeling
Since Jesus showed me the way.

"And how many *have* that satisfied feeling with Jesus in your heart," André asked the audience with the

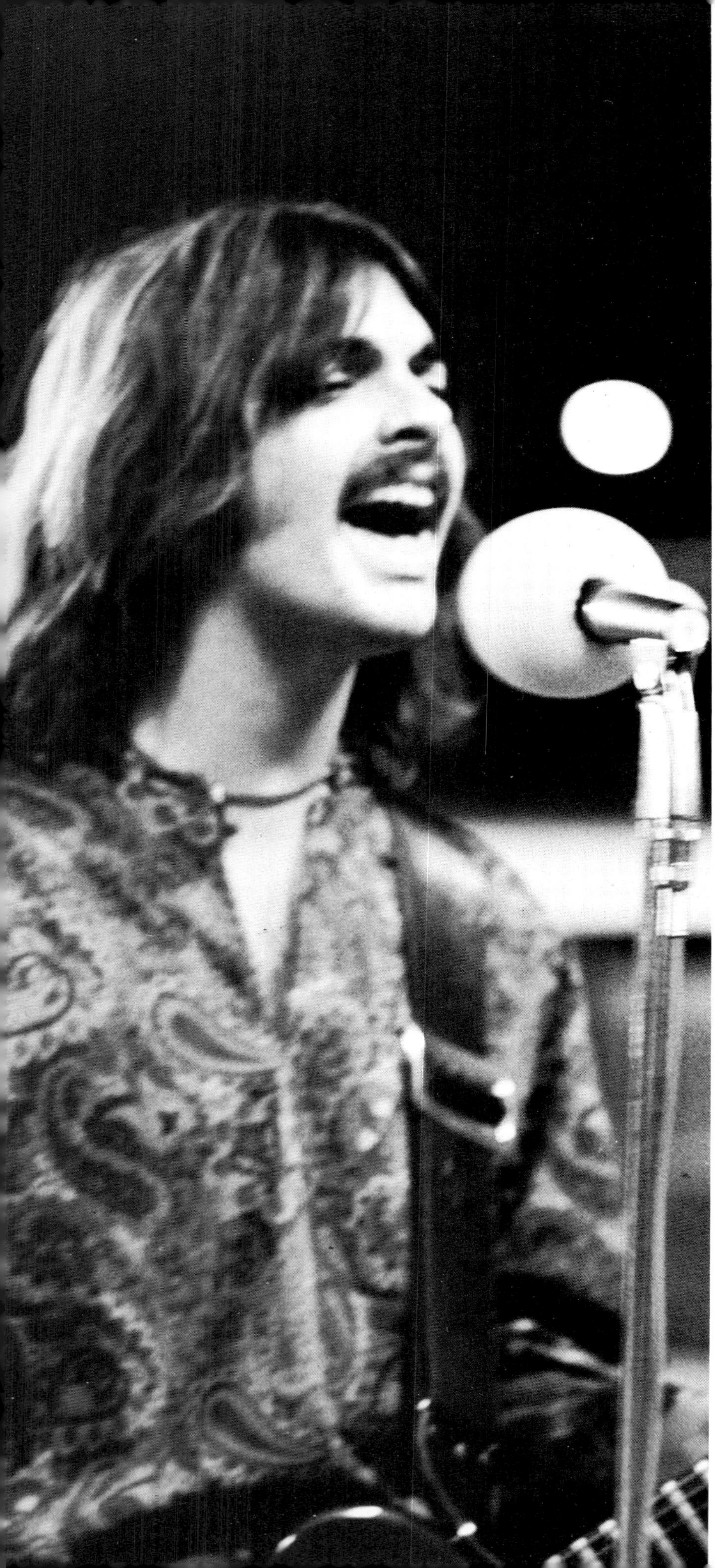

melodious singsong of a black revivalist. "Let me see your hands."

About eighty percent of the people in the room shot their hands up into the air, forefinger pointed skyward.

"Praise God," André said. "Because I trust you're not here just for the foot-stomping and the hand-clapping. We're here singing and talking about *Jesus*. That's something real. And it's too much sweat to be up here for something that's not real."

The audience agreed fortissimo, and the next song André sang, they sang along with him.

I went to another Jesus Music concert that was held in the 20,000-seat stadium of Cerritos College in Los Angeles. Only about five hundred people showed up for the music festival and I was told that it had been a little hastily put together and poorly publicized.

That, I thought, was a lousy excuse. Then I stopped to think when was the last time I remembered five hundred people coming out to hear Gospel music in my own home town, New York City. Not too often.

From the beginning, it's not difficult to tell the difference between a Jesus Music concert and a rock concert. A guy walks up to the center microphone.

"Testing, praise God. One. Two. Three. Testing."

And the people, they have a look about them. After a few numbers, when those few who had wandered into the concert thinking they were getting a free rock show started to leave, I looked at them and then at the people remaining. And there *was* a difference. The overall appearance might be the same—the remnants of hippiedom, but there really is that newly acquired gleam about them. It's a little indescribable, but unmistakable.

Meanwhile on the stage, one group after another took over the microphone. A group with a bluegrass sound called Kentucky Faith was there and so was Carrie's Company that I had seen in Melodyland. Then the Melodyland Drug Prevention Center's chorale, the Chromatics, took the stage.

Fifty young people—about half male and half female—standing proud. The girls wore colorful, ankle-length dresses, looking like young pioneer ladies on church day. The young men wore dress shirts, with the sleeves rolled up for that hot night. I recognized most of the Chromatics from the Melodyland services I had attended, and from the Hotline office I had spent a lot of hours in. They were like characters in a drama that was unfolding before me.

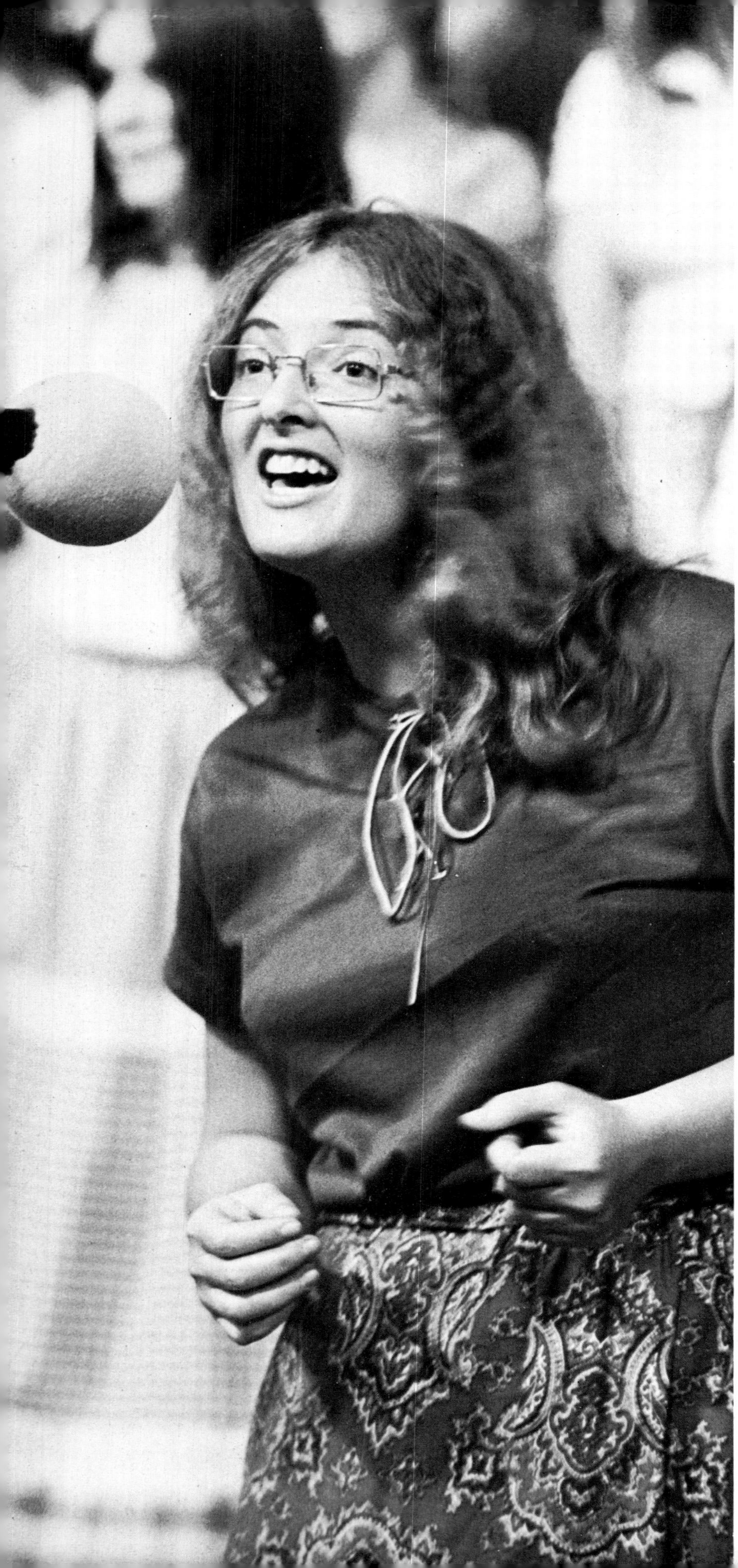

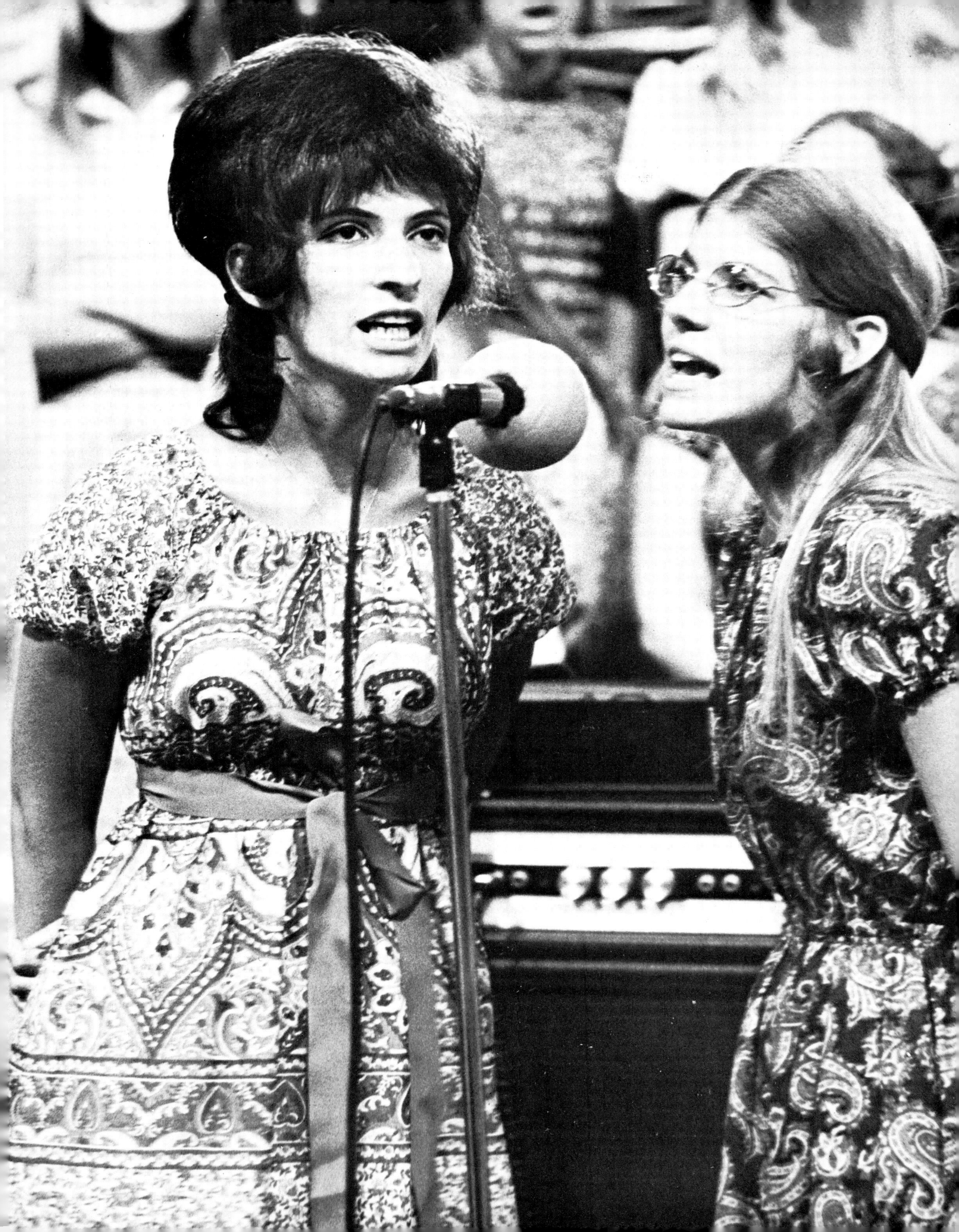

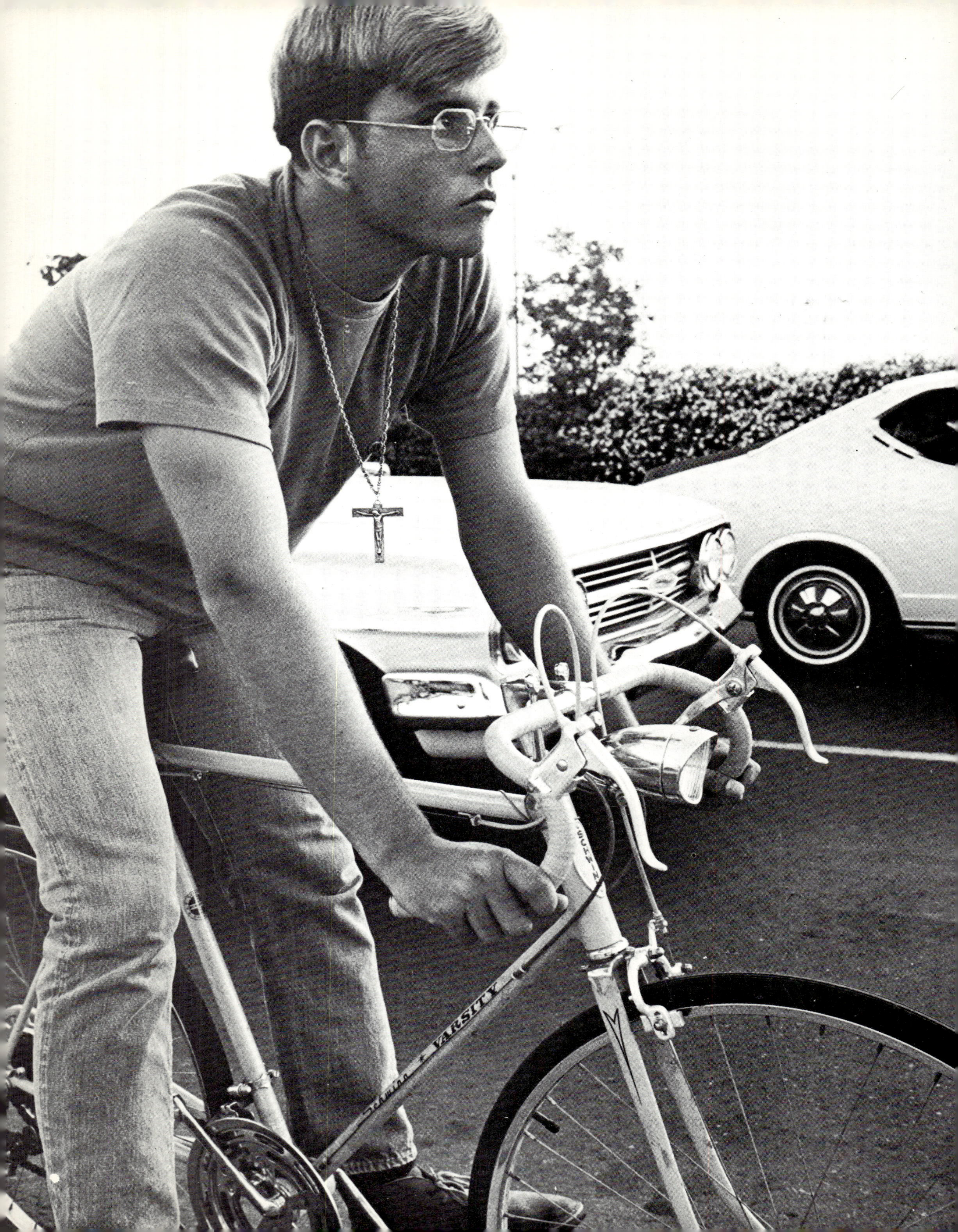
VARSITY

Donna was there, and Rod Walker, the eighteen-year-old gentle giant; Leslie Wakeling, the Center director's sprightly daughter; and Ron Winkler, the former acid freak turned charismatic master of ceremonies. And up to the center microphone came the group's soloist. She stood with her hands behind her back, and in a pure soprano, she sang a slow, earnest, and loving "Amazing Grace."

It gave me chills. It also struck me again how totally lives can change. Earlier, this same girl had told me that she had started smoking pot when she was fifteen, that she was into speed in her first year of college and dropping acid soon afterward. And here she was the centerpiece of a Jesus concert in front of five-hundred people, clean from drugs for over a year, "trying, I mean really *trying*, to walk with the Lord."

In the back row of the Chromatics, I saw another familiar face, Glen Blomgren, a twenty-year-old Marine sergeant. He was stationed in the El Toro Air Station in Santa Ana—twenty miles from the Chromatics headquarters at Melodyland. For some reason, he managed to make every rehearsal when he wasn't on duty and he also served a weekly shift as a Hotline volunteer. He made the forty-mile round trip several times a week, by bicycle. Not as penance, but pleasure.

"It takes me about two hours to make the trip," he had told me. "But I like it. You can get a lot of praying done when you spend four hours a day on a bicycle."

Glen had served in Vietnam. "I know for a fact that I killed men and I know my life was one endless trip looking for some kind of happiness through sex, or drinking, or drugs or anything.

"One time last year I got to go home on leave—I live in Waukegan, Illinois—and I saw that they had a Hotline. Same kind of setup as they have at Melodyland.

"So I went there, just to check it out, and I see a guy who was my best friend before I joined up, and he was a counselor there! I couldn't believe it. Here was a guy I had known all my life, and he had turned Christian!

"I didn't know what to say, but he started talking to me and telling me all the changes that had happened in his life and I was kind of wavering on the line.

"But then I thought no, since I had killed people in combat, God could never accept me. And my friend told me that was baloney, that the Lord was anxious for me to ask him into my heart.

"Finally he convinced me, and I asked Jesus into my

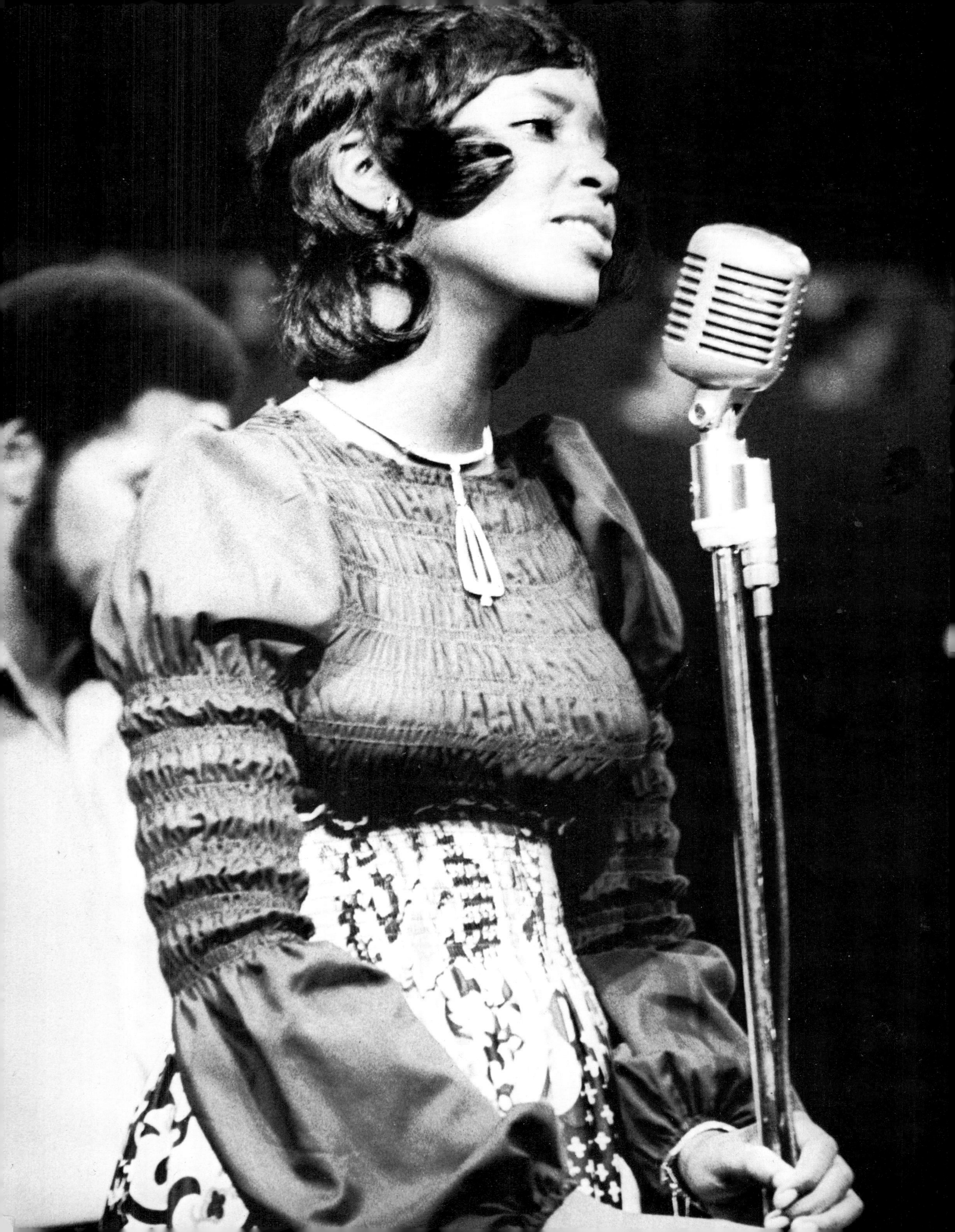

heart and right there, I knew that I was forgiven for everything. And it really blew my mind.

"A few days later, my leave was just about up, and my friend asked me if I had been filled with the Holy Spirit yet. And I said no, I didn't know what that was, so he and his girl friend took me out to his car and we all got into the back seat and they sat on either side of me. They were praying that I'd get the Baptism of the Holy Spirit, and I started asking for it too, and all of a sudden it was like my soul opened up. For ten minutes the Holy Spirit took hold of my tongue and I was speaking heavenly words I didn't even understand. There are no human terms that can describe the Baptism of the Holy Spirit. I think the only understanding can come through experiencing.

"For three days after that, I went around just smiling all the time. Then I had to go back to the base, and at first, people wouldn't believe the change in me. I was walking around happy and my language had cleaned up and I was just a different person.

"At first the guys rejected me—even my buddies. They kept cutting me down. But I just said 'God loves you anyway.' Now some of the guys respect my beliefs, and some others are even beginning to come around and ask questions.

"I've been a loudmouth all my life anyway. Now I just stand up and tell what the Lord's done for me. I know I'm a living testimony. It feels good."

A twenty-year-old Marine sergeant, humming "Amazing Grace" behind the soloist, who peddles forty miles on a bicycle every chance he gets so he can get away and pray, and then be with other young Christians, and who tells his Marine buddies that God loves them—*that* blew my mind.

I saw another face I recognized in the Chromatics choir. A young man whose head jerked in strange contortions and whose lips couldn't always form the right words when he sang.

He was born with cerebral palsy. His movements were spastic and his lips contorted painfully as he formed words.

I was told a story about him, and while I only want to write here what I heard and saw myself, this story has to be an exception.

Apparently the Chromatics had been invited to sing at the Nellis School for Boys in Whittier, California. I had heard of it, and I knew it had a tough crowd. It was not the kind of concert the Chromatics particularly enjoyed, but they went anyway, and for some reason, by no preplanning or conspiracy, the young man with the palsy came forth between songs to give witness.

The audience was merciless. As he told his story, how the Lord had changed his life and made him unafraid to face the world despite his handicap, his voice cracked with every several words and the jeers came with every crack. Some of the boys—who were in Nellis instead of jail only because of their age—did loud imitations of the young man. Others made grunting sounds, hooted, and whistled.

The young man kept speaking until he had completed his testimony, while the Chromatics stood behind him, their heads bowed in prayer.

When it was over, the choir had a few more songs they were scheduled to sing, and then they could leave—not soon enough. But just before the last song, a young, tough-looking black stood up in the back of the auditorium.

"I'm talking for the guys in cottage eight, and I'd like to say something to the fella' with the speech defect."

The young man walked forward to the center of the stage and said, "Yes?"

"Well, I can't speak for everyone," the black youth said. "But as for cottage eight, we want to apologize for the way we acted toward you. We were like animals and you were here just trying to help us and bring us something worthwhile. Speaking for my cottage, I want to say that I'm really sorry."

"We love you," the young Chromatic said evenly. Some of the singers began to cry, and some of the audience began to cry and the way I heard the story, about a dozen guys accepted Christ before the whole thing was over.

When the concert was over, George Wakeling, his wife Betty, and most of his large family—all members of the Chromatics—went out for a bite to eat. We were hungry, but before we began the meal, George led us in a prayer of thanksgiving. The restaurant was crowded and it was strange how people react to a family with their heads bowed over food, saying grace.

They pretend it's not happening.

People were looking up at the ceiling, or down at the

floor or out the window or at anything but us. It was as if they were embarrassed, but I didn't know for whom. I decided to stop looking around and get my head bowed. I was proud to be at the table no one wanted to see.

The Wakeling family is probably like most of the new Christian families—only possibly a little larger. George and Betty have two children and six boarders, including Donna, Rod Walker, and four other teenagers. They have arguments. They have jealousies. They occasionally tease each other and hurt each other's feelings. In other words, I suppose, they would seem pretty normal.

The difference, and one would have to say it's a pretty significant difference, is that everything in the family is centered around the person of Jesus Christ and the practice of Christianity.

One evening when I was visiting, the phone rang every half-hour or so. Every call was for Suzy, a pretty blonde sixteen-year-old who had become a Christian about a year earlier.

"We're waiting for a birth," Betty Wakeling told me after about the fourth time Suzy was called to the phone.

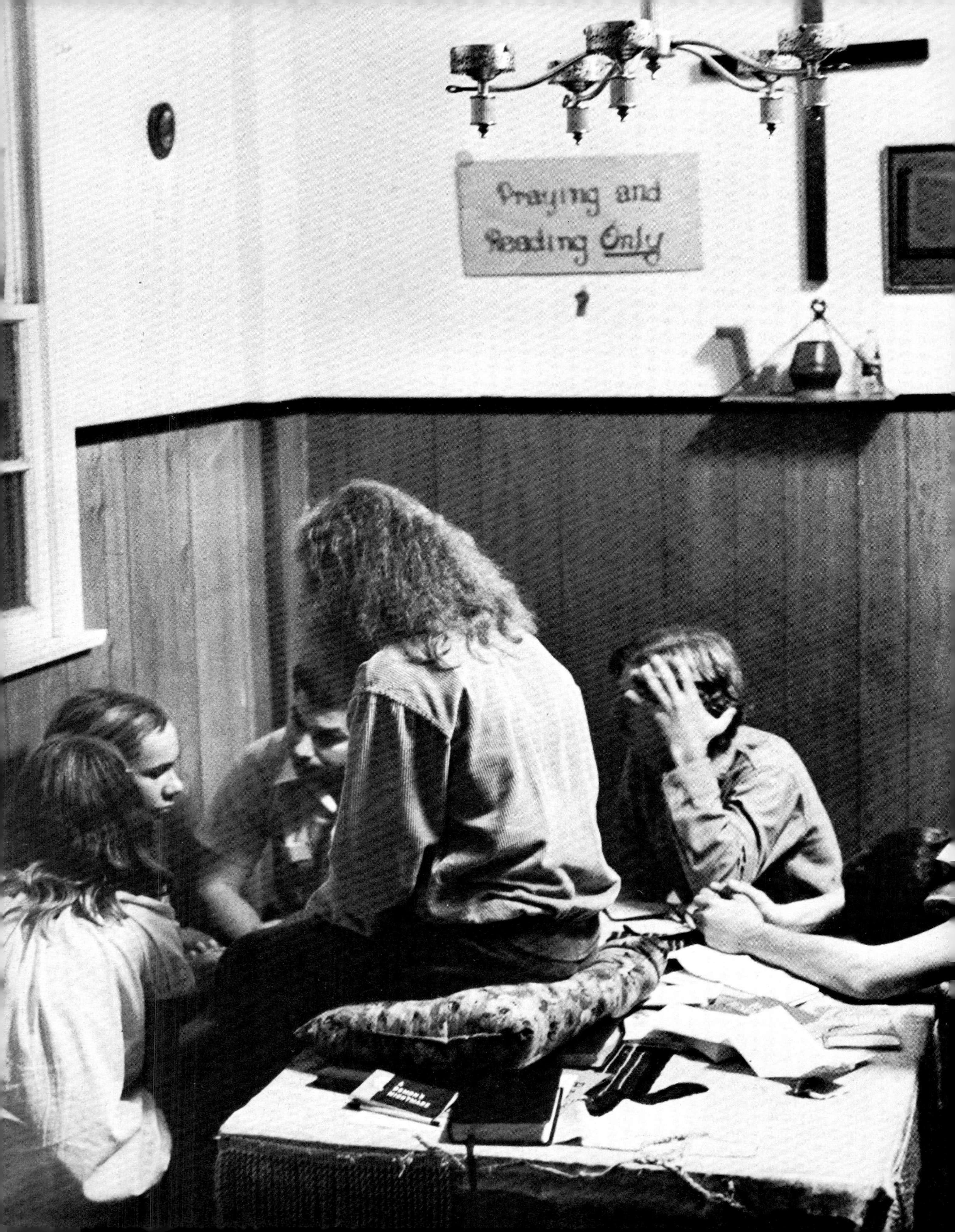
Praying and
Reading Only

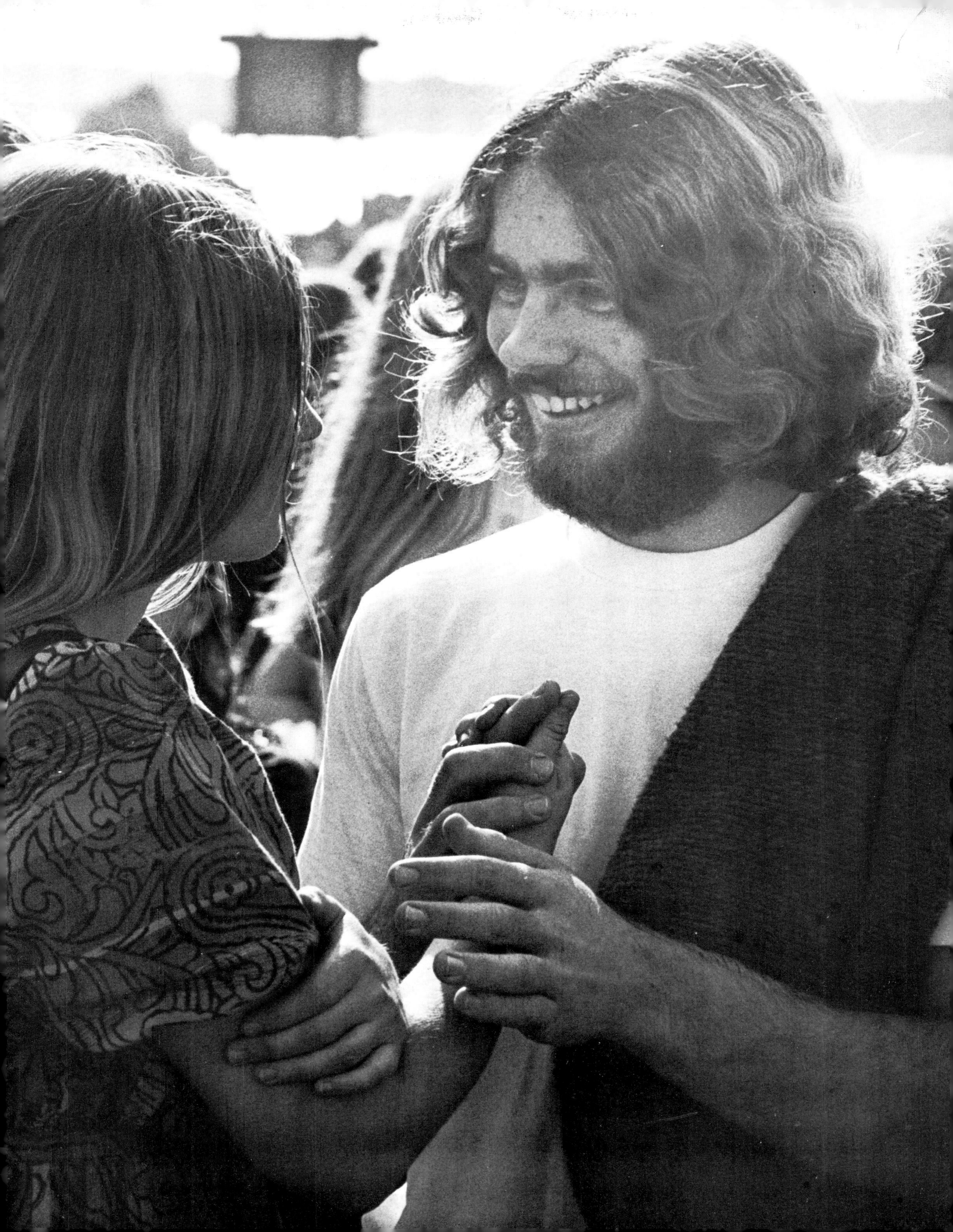

"Someone's having a baby?" I asked.

"It's a spiritual birth," Betty said. "One of Suzy's girl friends is getting very close to making a decision for Christ. We've been praying for her, and I guess we all know she's going to make it. But it's just coming slowly. She keeps calling Suzy asking more questions."

Then Suzy came into the room and everyone looked at her in anticipation.

"Yet?" somebody asked.

Suzy shrugged and held two fingers about half an inch apart. "This close," she said.

The room sighed, a little impatiently.

Dinner began, as do virtually all family functions at the Wakeling household, with a prayer. Then we started eating and the conversation turned—perhaps predictably—to the subject ever at hand: Christ. God. Eternity. But it was mostly my fault. I had some questions to ask too.

"What's this Jesus watch you're all wearing," I asked George. "Isn't that a little too gimmicky?" The watch has a small caricature ghost—signifying the Holy Ghost—on its face and its arms are the watch's hands. The inscription below the little caricature reads: "One Way." It was being sold out of the Melodyland book shop, and I had noticed that many members of the youth congregation were wearing it.

"It's a small thing, but it pulls people together," George said. "And it helps open doors. Anything that will get a conversation started about the Lord is okay with me."

Later, Donna was talking about her day—she had been invited to address the local chapter of the Lion's Club.

"I get tired of doing this—telling the mistakes I made in my life—and I've been doing it for two years. I told them that, how tiring it was to give my testimony day after day after day when I knew that ninety-six percent of the people I was talking to would walk out the door and not remember a word I said.

"But I said to them, I said if one person, one person is affected in one small little way by what I say, then it's really worth it for me."

"You really told them that?" George asked. Donna nodded proudly. "Good girl," he said.

When the dinner was coming to a close, Rod asked if he could be excused. He had a date. As he was walking out the door, a chorus at the table shouted out to him, "Proverbs thirty-one, Rod. Proverbs thirty-one."

Then they all laughed at their little joke. When we

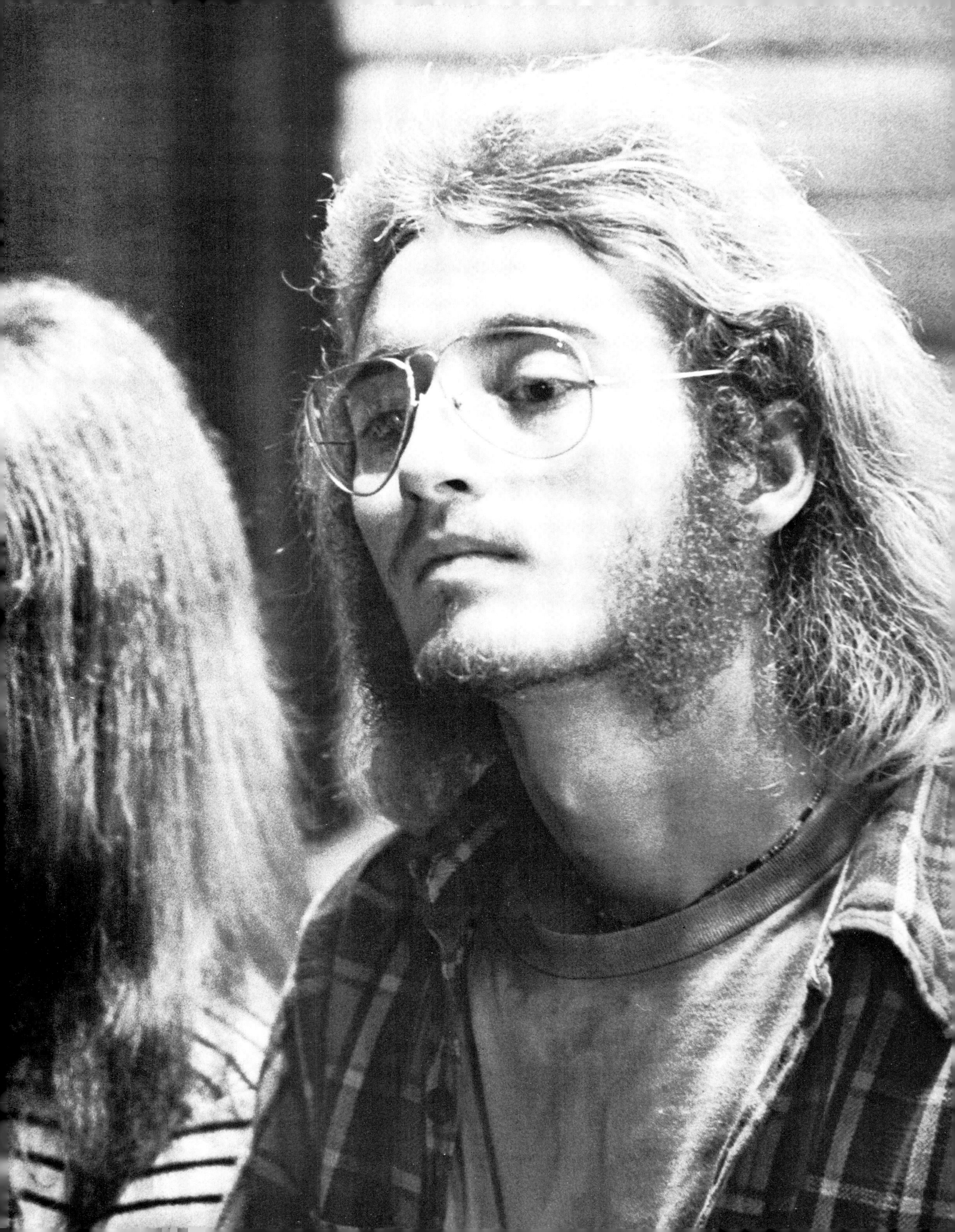

adjourned to the living room, I looked up verse 31 of Proverbs in the large Bible that dominated the coffee table. The verse had to do with picking a good wife. Even the humor at the Wakeling house is rooted to the lighter side of Christianity.

After a while it got time for me to leave, and George said he'd like to say a little prayer before I left. We all bowed our heads.

"Dear Lord," he began, "we thank you for this fellowship we had here this evening and we thank you for this wonderful day. We ask your blessing on every person in this room, and we especially thank you for letting Brian be with us this evening. We know that the article he did with Jack and Betty Cheetham brought thousands of people to Jesus and we pray this book they are doing will bring thousands more. We pray that you guide him in his writing, to glorify your name. We ask it in Jesus' name, Amen."

"Amen," the others agreed.

I thanked George for praying for me, and Betty for the wonderful meal, and then left for my motel. But I couldn't sleep that night. I kept thinking about George's words, and they disturbed me. I guess other people had said my article had been a blessing and had won converts to the Movement, but I carefully kept that kind of talk from getting lodged in my thoughts. I wanted to be just a reporter—I didn't want the responsibility of affecting someone's spiritual life.

But now it was lodged in my mind. What if that article had brought thousands of people into the Jesus Movement? What if those words and pictures were affecting people? I mean if there is a God in Heaven whose Son is Jesus Christ who died for our sins and then rose from the dead and ascended back into heaven, then okay. Fine. If I knew all that for a fact, then I'd be happy to do something to swing people into a revival. But none of those things had been categorically proven to me. It was okay for the Cheethams. They had been swept up. They were self-confessed members of the Movement.

But I wasn't. There was a lot about this revival I didn't particularly like and a lot more I didn't understand. Praying in tongues. Why would a God want his creation to worship him in indistinguishable sounds? And the Baptism of the Holy Spirit, that "indescribable experience." How many of those Baptisms were self-induced—subconscious drives into a state of ecstasy? And the Rapture.

Zap! Now you see me, now you don't. If that ever happened, who on earth, or who left on earth, could possibly resist becoming an instant convert? I just couldn't buy that whole package.

There were still too many things that just didn't sit right with me. What if Christianity is not the one true religion? What if it was just something Western Civilization dreamed up to keep the wheels of conscience turning? What if Jesus Christ was just a nice fellow, a good man who lived about 2,000 years ago and went around setting very good examples? What if the whole thing about him being raised from the dead was a big hoax—a rumor started by some over-zealous followers? And if that were true, and the divinity of Jesus was not, then wasn't the reporting we were doing pretty risky, helping to lead kids into a mammoth waste of time? Or even if it was just one kid. Did I want to be responsible for so much as one person devoting the rest of his or her life to a hoax?

I think these were the kinds of thoughts and questions I had been pretty strenuously avoiding for the past couple of months. Now that I wasn't avoiding those specific issues any more, I wondered if maybe I should avoid the liabilities attached to them. I wondered if maybe I shouldn't drop the whole thing. Write some other book. Report some other phenomenon.

Not all the Christians I talked to in California shared identical beliefs, and some in the Movement openly disagreed with the tactics or methods or even beliefs of others. But on two points, there is absolute, unflagging agreement from all sides.

Point one: Jesus is the Son of God.

Point two: He is coming back to this earth soon. The end of the world is coming. Planet earth, as a home for humanity, has a lease coming up soon. Unrenewable.

Point one I figured was pretty much a matter of faith, but point two was something open to a little more study and speculation. If indeed this world doesn't have much time to go, Christians must believe that from Scripture, and I wanted to know a little more about the basis for that belief.

I was introduced to Ray Rempt, a 28-year-old Ph.D. in physics who also was one of the most widely respected Biblical scholars and teachers among the young in the Los Angeles area.

We talked for a while about the Jesus Movement ("Sure, some people are doing it just because it's the latest trip"), and about his degree from UCLA ("I picked physics because I figured that would be the greatest challenge"), and finally I hit him with my big question.

"Is the end of the world coming soon, the Second Coming and all that?" It's a funny question to ask, even to ask a Biblical scholar. But maybe not a physics major.

"There's no doubt about it," he said. "Take this Jesus Movement as one of your proofs. Acts 2:17: 'And it shall come to pass in the last days, saith God, I will pour out of my Spirit upon all flesh: and your sons and your daughters shall prophesy, and your young men shall see visions, and your old men shall dream dreams.'

"Or take Matthew, Chapter 24. 'Many false prophets shall rise and iniquity shall abound.' In California last year, there were more divorces than marriages. How's that for iniquity?

Ray spoke with a deep, fierce intensity, and he kept his large black Bible clutched in his hand. But he seldom looked at it. I think he had it memorized.

"Or take Matthew again: 'Nation shall rise up against nation, and kingdom against kingdom, and there shall be famines and pestilences and earthquakes, in various places.'

"Certainly there has never been a time when there has been more international hatred, more hunger, and more earthquakes. Or take Timothy, Chapter 4," Ray said, quickly thumbing through his Bible and then looking back at me with his blue eyes blazing. " 'Now the Spirit speaketh expressly, that in the latter times some shall depart from the faith, giving heed to seducing spirits, and doctrines of devils . . . Forbidding to marry and commanding to abstain from meats.'

"Look at all your young people who are getting into black magic these days. And look at all the communes where marriage is forbidden. Or the health food sects who won't eat meat.

"And just take a look at the prophet Ezekiel in the Old Testament talking about the restoration of Israel. The Bible's just filled with prophecy showing that Jesus will be coming in our time. I really feel in my heart that these are the last days."

Ray was certainly not the guy to talk to if you wanted to do some long-range planning. What he said troubled me. Troubled me because he wasn't ranting and raving about the end of the world, but stating without doubt or hesitancy that we all are coming to the last days.

On my own last day, the last day of talking to the new Christians in California, I went back inevitably (or predictably) to Melodyland to talk to a young minister who had been a highly recommended source on the Movement. He was Tom Brewer, a modishly attired, handsome 25-year-old who was called (for lack of a better title, he said) the college minister. It was easy to see why he was given that responsibility. He was obviously bright, and his conversation was a kind of Christian-casual, with an agreeable flexibility that I hadn't really heard before. "You don't believe that? Fine," he would say. "I happen to, but I certainly don't set myself up as the ultimate source of truth on these things."

We talked for the better part of four hours, and I stopped taking notes after about the first. The interview was converted pretty quickly into an exchange. We talked about the Jesus Movement in California and everywhere else it seemed to be springing up. Tom talked about the young people today who were the sons and daughters of parents raised during the Depression. "It's really incredible to watch," he said. "Seeing these kids turn away from the materialism they grew up with and start looking for acceptance and love and identity."

I asked him if that wasn't really what a lot of the new movement toward fundamentalist Christianity was all about—a way to identify and be identified. "I'm a Christian. Are you a Christian? Wow. Praise God." Sort of like, "I'm a Libra. You're a Sagittarius? Wow. That's heavy." And he agreed.

We kept talking and gradually we weren't talking about the movement any more but about God. Tom said that he thought God was a personality—an ultimate personality who naturally wanted another personality to share His Being. So He made creation; He created the universe, and then mankind in His image. I asked Tom if that meant the only living creatures made by God were on this earth, and he said no. "There could be a zillion other planets containing life. There's no way we can claim to be exclusive."

Then I got onto my own religious experience—how one by one, things I had been taught in school or from the pulpit didn't make sense for me anymore. But every once in a while, I said, I'd get very religious. "Dear Lord, if you help me find my wallet, I'll go to Mass twice a Sunday for the next six months." And I'd find my wallet, and pretty consistently, I wouldn't keep my promise.

"So if I'm going to believe in a God, He would have to have a real sense of humor."

"He does," Tom said. "He *would* have to have!"

The conversation went on into the late afternoon and slowly it became obvious that I was talking matter of factly about God with this young minister, and he wasn't trying to convert me. But at the same time, he wasn't giving me any resistance. It was as if the whole conversation had somehow been previously programmed—neatly tailored to satisfy my doubts about the existence of a Supreme Being and my relationship with Him.

For weeks, I had been listening to sermons and talks and raps about God and Jesus and the promises and Christianity until I was drugged by it all. I sometimes couldn't wait to get back to my motel at night to give all my attention to some blessedly inferior television late show.

Or other times, I'd say to myself—all right, I will decide to believe in Jesus as the Son of God. I'll decide that because it will please the people around me, or because it sure can't hurt anything and might even help. But those reasons didn't work, even when I wanted them to. You can't "decide" to believe that a man who lived 2,000 years ago was the Son of God sent to this earth to save mankind. That's not the kind of thing you go around making intellectual conclusions about.

But Tom was disagreeing now. "That's *just* what you do. You decide. And that becomes faith."

"Tom, that's what I've been hearing all my life. 'Faith, son. You must believe it on faith.' And I've just never been one of the lucky ones to have such a simple trust come to me."

"But what is faith?" Tom said. "It's certainly not something you ever earned. It begins as a decision. A person decides to believe. And then faith comes, and grows. It's a gift."

That made sense to me. Somehow it worked, just as that whole afternoon was filled with explanations or assurances or even disagreements which were putting all the loose or lost ends of my Christianity together again. Earlier, Tom had said he was a fundamentalist and a Pentacostal. "So you believe Adam and Eve were created in the Garden of Eden one day and there was no evolution?" I asked.

"Yes, I believe that," he said. "But it's all speculation. Evolution might have been a part of the creative process, and if a Christian believes that, it's certainly not going to mess up my fellowship with him."

We kept talking, about the world's shifting morality and about God's absolute distinction between good and evil. We talked about Jesus, and Tom said that God sent His Son—Himself—to this earth as a demonstration of His love, through Jesus' life of selflessness. Jesus was God's Being on earth, an emissary who man could understand, and relate to, and believe in. And he said that Jesus wanted believers to confess him before others; to demonstrate they believed and accepted God's love.

And that was coming through to me. All the words and phrases were ones I had heard all my life. But I kept thinking: why hasn't it ever been clear to me before? Why hasn't anyone ever really *explained* it?

Tom kept talking, but at some point I stopped listening. Finally I interrupted him, kind of abruptly.

"I'd like to do it. I want to accept Jesus Christ as my Lord and Savior."

Tom stopped short.

"But I have an ulterior motive," I said quickly. "I want to accept Jesus because I would like to spend my eternity with God. I don't really know Jesus. I can't feel him. But I want to accept him. Kind of a matter of eternal security."

"Great," Tom said. "I can dig that."

"So what do I do?"

"You talk to God," he said. "You just go ahead and do it."

I wasn't sure if I was supposed to look up, or get on my knees, or what. So I just sat there and spoke out loud. I started by saying that I knew I had lived a totally self-centered life. But I wanted to accept Jesus Christ as my Savior. And I believe in my heart that he died for my sins. "And please God, help me to live a life that is pleasing to you."

That was it. When it was over, I felt neither silly nor sanctified. I imagined that Tom would tell me to keep praying and keep trying to believe, and that eventually I would be accepted. He didn't. He looked at me and he was smiling. No, he was grinning.

"You're a Christian," he said. "You're saved."

"You mean that's all there is to it?" I was thinking of the conversions I had seen, and the cries of joy and the convulsions and the shouting and hugging. There was nothing really overpowering in what I was feeling. Relieved maybe, and a little confused. Determined, perhaps. But I didn't really feel as if anything overtly dramatic had happened to me. And I told him that.

"It says in the Bible that if you confess with your mouth and believe in your heart, you shall be saved," Tom said. "It's just that simple. You decided to believe. You're saved."

There is a Jesus Movement upon us. I saw it happening in chapels and street corners, campuses and communes in California. I've been reading about it happening all over this country and hearing about it happening all over the world. It's not a fad. It's a world revival. An old-time, fundamentalist, Jesus-as-personal-savior revival.

It has attracted young people by the hundreds of thousands. And the young are influencing their elders. And Jesus is becoming very much alive in the world. Praise God.

Q
248 VAC

Vachon
Time to be born

Date Due

MAY 5 1999			

WITHDRAWN
Earlville Free Library

EARLVILLE FREE LIBRARY
EARLVILLE, NEW YORK

BRO DART Printed in U.S.A.

A000360019874